Dancing Through Life

Billy Forsyth MBE

Dancing Through Life

Author: Billy Forsyth MBE

Copyright © Billy Forsyth MBE (2023)

The right of Billy Forsyth MBE to be identified as author of this work has been asserted by the author in accordance with section 77 and 78 of the Copyright, Designs and Patents Act 1988.

First Published in 2023

ISBN 978-1-915996-91-6 (Paperback)
978-1-915996-92-3 (Ebook)

Cover Design and Book Layout by:
White Magic Studios
www.whitemagicstudios.co.uk

Published by:
Maple Publishers
Fairbourne Drive, Atterbury,
Milton Keynes,
MK10 9RG, UK
www.maplepublishers.com

All photographs and images are from Billy Forsyth MBE's personal collection including photographs by Mark Owen

A CIP catalogue record for this title is available from the British Library.

All rights reserved. No part of this book may be reproduced or translated by any form or by any means, electronic or mechanical, including photocopying, recording or by any information storage and retrieval system without written permission from the author.

The views expressed in this work are solely those of the author and do not necessarily reflect the views of the publisher, and the publisher hereby disclaims any responsibility for them.

CONTENTS

1. There's even a Story about the Stories 5
2. Life Began in Bridge of Allan 7
3. Family Holidays when I was young. 15
4. My Earliest Memory 21
5. Starting Highland Dancing 23
6. I was a Voracious Reader of Everything 31
7. My Best Friend growing up 33
8. Mum when I was young 39
9. School Days 47
10. Childhood Toys 51
11. My Dad when I was Young 55
12. My Working Life 63
13. Overseas dancing trips back in the day 71
14. The Stone of Destiny - Any Connection? 79
15. The Caledonia Show Tours 83
16. My Favourite Music & Songs 95
17. Winning the World Highland Dancing Championship 99
18. 'The Shoes' From Whence They Came 105
19. Flying High with British Caledonian 109
20. My JFK Moment 115
21. Best photograph I've ever had taken? 119
22. RSOBHD Delegate, Chairman, President 123
23. Any serious accidents? 133

24. Scotdance Uncovered 137
25. Meeting Famous or Important People 139
26. Using the Mortgage Money 155
27. Taking After Mum or Dad? 159
28. Joining the Military 161
29. What invention has had the biggest impact on your day-to-day life? 177
30. My Royal Connections 181
31. Memories of my Young Family 191
32. A Love Affair with The Cowal Highland Gathering 197
33. Tracing My Family Ancestry 203
34. What advice would you give your great-grandchildren 205
35. On Tour with The Vale 207
36. My proudest moment in life? 215
37. A lazy day at home? 217
38. The country has changed during my lifetime 219
39. Memorable Favourite Trips 223
40. How should I be Remembered? 233
41. A Timeline 235
42. The Author 243

1
There's even a Story about the Stories

A few years ago, I was having lunch in a South Bank, Brisbane, restaurant with a good friend, Margaret Paterson, a highly qualified and respected teacher of highland dancing, who lives in one of the suburbs of Brisbane in Queensland, Australia. Margaret and I are somewhat similar in age (OK she is younger) and I knew and had greatly respected Margaret's mother, Innes Barker, another great highland dance teacher and judge, who had befriended me years before on my various trips to Australia. Our lunches had become a 'must do' thing whenever I was in Queensland or Margaret was in Scotland.

As always, the conversation covered everything from families and friends to highland dancing events and the problems of the world in general. At one point she mentioned that she had written, for every year of her life, a note about something that had happened to or about her in that year.

On my return home I thought about that and decided I could do the same. I collected my thoughts and looked through the mass of paperwork and photographs I had accumulated over the years, two full four- drawer filing cabinets of it. I managed to cover most of the significant moments and events and found that there were many more than a single story to write up for each year.

On a more recent trip I gave Margaret a copy of my lists and asked her for comments. Her remarks were a bit brutal, but truthful.

Dry as dust. No emotion. A series of dates and places. No colour to it at all. Not a good sign.

As it happens, for my Christmas present a year back, the Flying Circus, otherwise known as my son Colin, wife Nic, and children Ballagh, Lachie, Eilidh, Rannoch and Aoife, gave me a subscription to a company who produce hardbound books consisting of stories written by older members of families, recalling their adventures over the years for their children and grandchildren, to make sure those stories are remembered and not forgotten. A book of memories of how things were at a different time and in a different age.

Every week or so Colin would send me a new subject to write about, with the idea that after a full year they would take all those stories and publish them in a book.

It has not been an easy year for many, many reasons, and it wasn't long before I was way behind in my writing. To be honest, some five or six, then about ten or twelve weeks behind. I have made a determined effort and at last I am catching up with the program.

So everything has been revamped, rewritten and a bit of 'colour' added for good measure.

Denise says she has become a 'Story Widow' while I hide away writing up my memories.

Hope you all (and Margaret) enjoy the results.

2

Life Began in Bridge of Allan

My Mum and I lived in a one-bedroom flat (the traditional Scots 'Room and Kitchen') above Tommy Hardie's pub 'The Rising Sun' in New Street, Bridge of Allan. My Dad was on active service in the Royal Corps of Signals mainly in North Africa then over to Sicily and on to the mainland of Italy.

The flat had a bedroom facing over New Street and a triangular shape kitchen/sitting room with a window looking down the alley behind the Pub towards Allanvale Road. There was a toilet but no bathroom and I remember the big tin bath being filled with hot water for the weekly bath and hair washing. Gas lighting and cooking was normal and woe betide you if you damaged the gas 'mantle' before it was attached and lit.

Mr. & Mrs. Maclaren lived down the street, Grannie Hamilton lived across the street on one side of a narrow alleyway off New Street with Mr. & Mrs. Millar on the other side of the alley. Mrs. Eadie and an older guy with a gammy leg, Mr. Anderson, who drove a local taxi, lived in the building opposite the pub. Mrs. Marshall and Jimmy lived round the corner on Allanvale Road. Teenagers Frances and Margaret Maclaren and Margaret Hamilton were apparently often babysitters for me.

Cousins Buildings on the opposite side of the road contained a number of flats accessed from closes/staircases off the street. Ex-marine captain Bill Maclaren ran the tobacconists on the corner of New Street and Henderson Street with Davy the Butchers on the opposite corner. Bill Jackson (also known as Richardson) ran the corner shop at the bottom of New Street (later he moved the shop to Henderson Street opposite New Street).

Mathieson the Bakers, Mrs. Dick's fruit and veg shop and the Queens Hotel were along Henderson Street towards the Clock, just before Queens Lane, which led down to Allanvale Road past the local volunteer Fire Brigade Station and Turnbull's Bacon Factory.

The Allan Water Café and chip shop, run by Louis Togneri was on the north side of Henderson Street just before Blairforkie Drive and the old Bridge over the river.

When I was old enough (probably about 5 yrs.) I remember regularly running along Henderson Street to the Coop (locally called 'the Store') in the morning for our breakfast rolls and milk. 'Bessie' seemed to be in charge of the 'Store' as she was responsible for taking the money.

Our play areas were the Street and the washing green/waste ground off Allanvale Road outside Jimmy's house. There I recall we used chairs a lot, in a row with upturned pram wheels at the front, our bus, or over our shoulders, as Pipers in a Band. Long sticks were held across our body and thrown in the air as Drum Majors with the Pipe Band.

My mother was a regular visitor to Glasgow for shopping and for entertainment and every year she would take me to 'Jeromes' the photographers in a semi basement studio on Argyll Street for the 'annual photo'. This is probably the first one taken.

In 1944 I started dance classes with Margaret Mason in Keirfield Cottages, Bridge of Allan. Margaret had been a pupil of Bobby Cuthbertson so had been taught well.

The cottage was near the Keirfield Dye Works with access on a track past the main factory entrance or by a path from the bottom of Fountain Road, across the river (the White bridge which is now Blue). The cottages were demolished and that path closed many years ago to allow expansion of the factory. By law an alternative path had to be provided so what is now known as the 'Chicken Run' was provided.

Dad returned from active military service with Royal Corps of Signals in 1945. He started work again as a neoprene Hose maker at Forthvale Rubber Works, Cornton Road, Stirling.

We moved to a new house at 20 Cawder Gardens, Bridge of Allan. A new post-war development of 28, 4 in a block, houses in an oblong layout with a grassed area in the centre. Now we have three bedrooms upstairs, with an entrance hall, bathroom, sitting room, kitchen and scullery downstairs. We also had a front and rear garden to set up.

Behind the house beyond the back garden was a field used for crops and sometimes to graze cattle. The opposite side of the field was bounded by the main railway line from central Scotland to Oban in the West, Perth and Inverness in the North and Dundee and Aberdeen in the East. Although there was a great amount of regular traffic on this line, passenger and freight, after a while we just didn't hear it, though all our visitors said they did. After a couple of nights they too forgot about it.

The Cheethams lived at No.19, the Campbells at No.18 on one side, the MacKenzies at No.21 and the Mitchells at No.22 on the other side. The central grassed oval was our playground, football pitch and general community use area.

In 1947 I started competing on a fairly regular basis travelling all around Central Scotland.

At this time my mother started writing a list of medals won in an old heavy black cover Exercise Book. She kept this going, incorporating press cuttings from the Stirling Newspapers, until 1960.

My Mum and Dad were both keen cyclists and before they were married, members of their local cycling clubs as were most of their brothers and sisters. They met through the 'club runs' the regular Sunday touring days out that had up to 50 club members cycling off to the lochs and glens of central Scotland in all weathers. For many years the 'drumming up' spots along the roads of Stirlingshire, Fife, Perthshire and even further afield were pointed out to me along with the reasons why they were suitable, a bridge to shelter under if it rained, a burn for fresh water for making tea on the primus stove etc.

September 1946 My first outfit and medals

During the Second World War my dad was a driver with 7th Air Formation Signals Regiment in North Africa, Sicily and Italy so after returning home he was keen to find a car to get us around.

The 1936 Morris 8 wasn't exactly luxurious but it was easier than buses and trains. There was a lot of maintenance required and it eventually ground to a halt near Crossgates in Fife and was dispatched to the scrap yard.

With so many relatives in Fife we spent a lot of time visiting there, staying at our Grandad and Grannies house at 37 Denfield Avenue in Dundonald. It was a short walk from there round to Auntie Agnes Jameson's in Cardenden, and a ten-minute journey to Uncle Jock's in Kirkcaldy. Auntie Mary and Uncle Ted Morgan, Ivor, Blair and Nan were in Dunfermline as were Auntie Katie and Uncle Billy Morgan (Ted's brother) and their girls Gwen and Evelyn. Auntie Peggy and Uncle Bobby Wise with Alex, Sandra and William lived in Glenrothes. Auntie Frances and Uncle David MacVicar lived in Cowdenbeath. There were another two unmarried Aunts, Nina who was ill for many years with suspected Tuberculosis, and Auntie Lizzie who was near Cupar.

In these quieter times it was possible for me to take Andrea on our own to our Grannies without any problems, I would have been about 12 or 13 yrs. old. We caught the bus from Bridge of Allan to Causewayhead roundabout and transferred there to the Dunfermline bus. We had a choice of route via Blairhall or via Kincardine whichever bus came first. In Dunfermline bus station (now the site of a supermarket) we took the Lochore bus as far as Lochgelly, getting off at Auchterderran Road, at the top of the Liza Brae. That was the first time I came across a double decker bus with wooden slatted seats. They were regular on that route. That final bus took us through the Jamphlars, Auchterderran and Bowhill where we finally left it at the bottom of Station Road and walked up the hill past the station to Dundonald and Denfield Avenue.

The Forsyth Family Grandkids circa 1949 – Jamesons, Forsyths, Morgans and Wises

For the first few years, when we were in New Street, Mum went back on a Sunday to services at the Murrayfield United Free Church in Bannockburn at the Cross, opposite the Town Hall. I attended Sunday school there for a short time. When we moved to Cawder Gardens I went to Sunday School at Lecropt Kirk for a time then to Chalmers Church on Henderson Street.

My only real memory of being in Grannie Stevenson's house in Maitland Avenue, Bannockburn was playing with the next-door neighbour's daughter Jean Scott. She was the same age as me, apparently a cutey and obviously my first girlfriend. Apart from a few photos I don't have any memory of Grandad and Grannie Stevenson, apart from the fact that he bred Canaries, and was well known for that.

My Uncle Jimmy Stevenson, Auntie Jean, Big Billy, Margaret and Jim lived in Cochrie Place, Tullibody on the edge of the wood. Uncle Jimmy worked at the Cambus Distillery and it became a traditional January 1st visit for all the Stevenson families. Nothing to do, of course, with the bottles of strange clear liquids which were dispensed to the adult male members at that party. The ladies were more likely to have 'a small sherry', maybe even with lemonade. His son Billy was a few years older than me and taller hence the 'Big' Billy, 'Wee Billy' nicknames.

Grandad & Grannie Stevenson with Uncle Wullie

Uncle Andrew Stevenson, another Auntie Jean with Lottie (Charlotte) and Drew (Andrew) lived in Stirling. Uncle Andrew played drums in a Dance Band around the local area.

Uncle Wullie Stevenson lived in Bannockburn with Auntie Maisie, Marion and Tommy.

Auntie Helen Stevenson lived in a Care Home in Dundee and we went there a couple of times a year.

That's a lot of family and a lot of cousins to keep up with, so don't even try to work out who's who.

Life Began in Bridge of Allan

3
Family Holidays when I was young.

My Mum and Dad were both keen cyclists and before they were married, members of their local cycling clubs as were most of their brothers and sisters.

During the Second World War my dad was a driver with 7th Air Formation Signals Regiment in North Africa, Sicily and mainland Italy so after returning home he was keen to find a car to get us around.

The 1936 Morris 8 wasn't exactly luxurious but it was easier than buses and trains. There was a lot of maintenance required and it eventually ground to a halt near Crossgates in Fife and was dispatched to the scrap yard.

It was followed by a 1938 Morris 10 which lasted a lot longer.

Those cars took us to visit friends and relatives, travel round the Highland Games and go on holiday all over Scotland.

Holidays were spent camping.

Scotland was barely out of the war years and food rationing was still ongoing however as a long-time cycling nation everyone was used to travelling light and making the best of what little we had. The camaraderie of the cycling clubs transferred easily to the camping community and everyone gave a helping hand if problems arose.

Family Holidays when I was young.

Camping at the side of Loch Lomond 1947 - Drum up time on A9 near Kingussie 1948

I remember my early years in a tent on the grassy slopes of Loch Lomondside, just beyond Luss, where there was an explosion of campers during the annual Glasgow Fair Fortnight as it was easy to reach by bus and train from the city centre. Campers had simple needs, a tent to sleep in, fresh water (Loch Lomond did and still provides Glasgow's drinking water) and a primus stove to heat the soups and stews and brew the tea.

Scotland has always had an enlightened approach to use of the countryside and what is now called 'wild camping' was the norm back then. Unfortunately, in recent times 'wild camping' has attracted a young, uncaring element who seem only interested in freedom to drink alcohol, cut down woodland to make campfires and leave their rubbish behind when they leave, thus having no respect for the environmental problems they cause. In the 1940s those problems were little known and with only a few cars on the roads the camping fraternity were still mainly cyclists or hill walkers.

We camped regularly at Seafield on the outskirts of Kirkcaldy, collecting sea coal from the beach to make our campfires and searching the water's edge and sand dunes for fishes and beasties. It was an easy run from Bridge of Allan and the nearest access point for us to the sea. The North Sea is not known for warm temperatures but we paddled along the beach in all weathers though it must have been cold.

I remember our car being unable to drive up the hill on the outskirts of Aberdour (even a cyclist could ride up it) and my dad turning the car round and going up in reverse gear as it was a lower ratio than the first gear on the car. How things change.

Travelling around Scotland to the Highland Games we made camp in all sorts of locations from Ganavan Sands, outside Oban, to the Fife coast villages.

In the 1940s and 1950s the main summer holiday period for most Scots was the 'Trades Fortnight' when most businesses in an area shut down completely for two weeks.

It began with the Scottish Borders in June, moved to the Edinburgh area for the first fortnight in July then to Glasgow and the West of Scotland for generally the second fortnight of July.

Because of the varying 4 or 5 weekends in July I was always told 'the Glasgow Fair Fortnight starts on the first Monday after the Second Tuesday in July'. I don't know who came up with this calculation but I have never known it to fail to prove correct.

Into August and the holiday period moved north to Perth and Angus then to Aberdeenshire and on to Inverness and North West Highlands. It's probably no coincidence that the Border Ridings, Highland Games and Agricultural Shows were held during those times in the different parts of the country. For the North and North West of Scotland it also coincided with the migration of landed families returning to their ancestral (or new-money purchased) homes for the Hunting, Shooting and Fishing Season with house parties all over the Highlands. The Argyllshire Gathering was the last Thursday of August and the Royal Braemar Gathering the first Thursday of September, both events part of 'the season' and graced by Royalty and such like families in the area.

It was not until 1959 that we took the plunge to try camping in France. It was a new experience for us and we found that the campers on the Continent took full advantage of the better and more consistent warm weather to really expand their camping facilities. It was also a new experience in our travel arrangements too. My folks had found an 'air ferry' service on the south coast of England so we flew with the car on a big box-like aircraft from

Lydd Airport near Romney Marsh to Le Touquet on the French coast, it must have taken all of 20 mins in the air.

No images of our little Austin A40 Farina loading up have been found though some must exist somewhere.

We travelled from Le Touquet to Paris to do some sightseeing before moving on towards the Mediterranean coast. My sister Andrea says we spent her 13th birthday in Paris camping in the Bois de Boulogne, almost in the city centre. In those days the great tourist bibles were the Michelin Guides which gave an amazing amount of information and travel directions within their green covers. We had the general one for France and the detailed one for Paris itself.

Saint-Aygulf was a revelation for us who were used to camping, often in wind and rain, in Scotland. The warm water of the Mediterranean Sea and constant sunshine – Bliss for a whole week. The tents, some more like small bungalows, had so many amenities attached. Outdoor kitchens were normal and many campers obviously spent a long time there as they had little fences around their tents and bunting decorated their lounge areas.

Language was a bit of a problem at times. On the road south we stopped for a meal which I ordered in my best schoolboy French. Not quite what we expected as a thick stew appeared followed by another 'main course' of indeterminate materials. All part of the experience I suppose.

During our time on the coast, we visited other towns and villages including Nice and Cannes and a trip to the famous Monte Carlo in the Principality of Monaco.

As an aside, on the return journey north, our last stop was in a forest campsite near Rheims, north east of Paris. On the same site was a school group from Nottingham also on their way home from a camping holiday in France. In chatting to some of the group I ended up exchanging details with a girl called Diane who lived on Wilford Lane, on the south side of Nottingham.

A year later my friend Ian and I dropped in to visit Diane on our way south for a dancing championship in Somerset. It's enough to say Ian and Diane ended up rather the worse for wear after a few libations and her friend Anne and I sorted them out and spent most of the evening talking to each other while doing so. We hit it off rather well and kept in touch.

Diane, Anne & Billy in Wilford Lane, Nottingham 1960

Our last holiday as a family was in 1960 when we spent three weeks on the continent, mainly in Italy, but travelling up through Austria and Germany before returning on the Ferry from Zeebrugge in Belgium. We took the ferry from Hull to Zeebrugge, transferred from there to the overnight train car ferry which landed us the following morning in Milan, Italy. First time for us to use Couchettes, the beds which folded down from the back wall of our compartment. After a brief tour round Milan, we made for the Mediterranean coast city of Genoa. From there we drove south stopping off in Florence and Pisa (for the Leaning Tower) before heading for Rome.

The camp site there was on the outskirts of the city and had a small café where Andrea and I tried plates of real Italian spaghetti. Our efforts caused some laughter from the Italians watching us who quickly gave us a lesson in how to twist a forkful of spaghetti

Family Holidays when I was young.

against a spoon then pop the lot in our mouths. We visited all the places I had read about in the High School Latin class, the Colosseum, the Senate, St Peter's in the Vatican and the Circus Maximus where the famous chariot races were held.

From Rome we crossed to the Italian east coast on the Adriatic Sea then north to Bologna, Padua and Venice. I remember walking in St Mark's Square and watching the Gondoliers do their stuff on the canals but the cost of a trip on one was too much for our budget.

From Venice we travelled north into Austria then into Germany where we camped in the village of Oberammergau where every ten years the villagers perform 'The Passion Play', the story of Christ and his Crucifiction, as a thank you for the survival, in the Middle Ages, of the local people from the plague which was rampant across Europe. We were lucky to get tickets for a performance, which lasted all day, however as this was in German a lot went over our heads.

From there we drove across Germany and back to Zeebrugge in Belgium for the ferry back to UK.

4
My Earliest Memory

I have many memories of my younger days but, apart from having photos taken by family, and in Jerome's studio on Argyle Street in Glasgow, I think my earliest memory was probably of cycling down New Street in Bridge of Allan on my little three-wheeler trike, my legs working hard pushing the pedals on the front wheel.

Although that is the memory I have, the only clear photo I can find is one taken in the Pullar Park. About that same time when my Aunt Mary (Dad's sister) visited there is another one where it was festooned with flags for some sort of children's event in the village. As always for those events I was wearing a kilt and balmoral bonnet. That photo seems to have been taken outside the flat in New Street based on the stone wall in the background. I would have been probably age 3 at the time so the summer of 1944

The Trike and ready for a Parade with Auntie Mary

Although this was a three-wheel trike and both parents were keen cyclists I never actually owned a bicycle when I was young as my Mum always said the leg muscles used for cycling were not the ones I used for dancing and wouldn't buy me a bike.

The other photo I have found taken at a similar age was at another children's parade in Bridge of Allan when I was driving a small four-wheel car dressed overall with Lion Rampant flags.

Note the Argyll cap badge which at that time was solid silver, and the 1/3 pint of milk I was drinking, a regular issue to schoolkids at that time, it was continued through Primary school; and of course, I was already used to wearing a kilt.

Sometime later that year the Argyll cap badge was lost on a walk up the glen in Bridge of Allan and despite searching high and low it was never found.

As you will appreciate with the UK waging a war in Europe the village was always raising funds for the war effort and keeping families and children involved by holding many events for them, indoors in winter and outdoors during the summer months.

The Pullar Park (known to us as the Memorial Park because of the cenotaph) was well used as was the Museum Hall on Henderson Street and the Masonic Hall on Union Street.

5
Starting Highland Dancing

Mum had always been a keen dancer, Old Tyme, as it was known, a mixture of ballroom round the room sequence dances and Scottish social dances. She had never had formal training so at 3 yrs. old I was sent along to the local dancing teacher.

Margaret Mason taught in the backroom of Keirfield Cottage (since demolished), her home which was on the far side of the River Allan, over the white metal bridge where Allanvale Road and Fountain Road met up. Margaret had been a pupil of Bobby Cuthbertson, one of the best Highland Dancers ever, so had been taught well and was passing on her knowledge to the local kids.

This photo was taken in 1945 and includes many well-known local residents, many still live in the area.

During the time I was there she held concerts for parents and friends usually in the Museum Hall on Henderson Street, and included in addition to Highland Dances many so called 'fancy dances', such as the Dutch Clog and Polish Mazurka. How traditional they were I don't know but they filled out the programme.

From my limited memory it was not until my dad was demobbed that we started going to dancing competitions. 1947 was the year I started competing on a fairly regular basis travelling all around Central Scotland.

Many competitions took place indoors in Coatbridge run by a woman called Jenny Imrie, who was also the main person behind a local all-girls pipe band called The Braemar Ladies Pipe Band. To get to those events we took an Alexanders Bluebird bus towards Glasgow changing at the crossroads in Condorrat (just beyond Cumbernauld village) to a local service from Kilsyth for the trip cross country to Coatbridge.

Most of the competitions were either indoor events run by individuals, or Community Gala Days or small local Highland Games. Neilston, near Glasgow, Newtongrange near Edinburgh and Salsburgh, Whitburn and Bathgate between Glasgow and Edinburgh were also competition venues.

At this time my mother started writing a list of medals won in an old heavy black cover Exercise Book. She kept this going, incorporating press cuttings from the Stirling and other newspapers, until about 1960. At Cowal Highland Gathering, I was awarded the 3rd place medal in the Sword Dance, the Judge was Bobby Cuthbertson who had taught my teacher Margaret Mason. Thus started a link with the Gathering which has lasted to the present day. Dancer, Judge, Host and Commentator over the years.

Dancing Through Life

That year I also danced at the Royal Braemar Gathering for the first time, in front of the Royal Pavilion where not only King George VI and his family sat, but also Queen Mary, widow of King George V.

I think because of my size I appeared in numerous Press photos, and was filmed for Pathe News, which was shown in Cinemas all over the United Kingdom.

When I was 10 years old my Mum decided I would progress better with a male dance teacher and she was advised to contact Willie Cuthbertson in Glasgow. Willie was the younger step brother of Bobby Cuthbertson but, during his competitive days, he had danced under his middle name, Willie McNiven so all his trophies were held under that name. He had only a small group of dancers, many of them boys, whom he taught in the large front room of his house in Clayton Terrace in Dennistoun.

Starting Highland Dancing

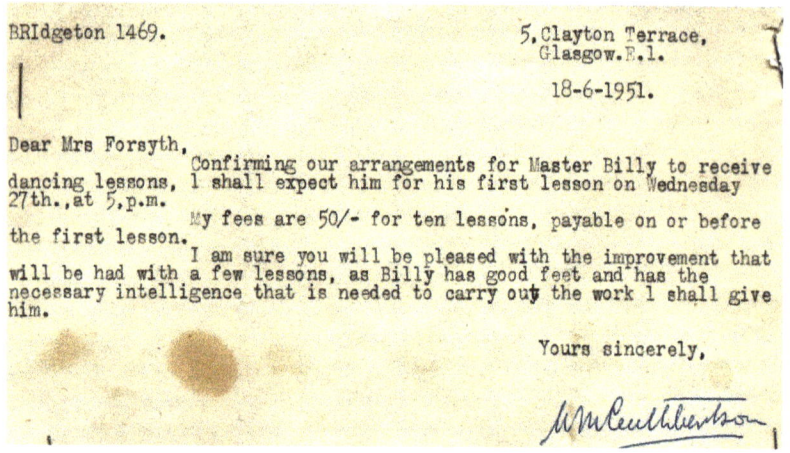

All the years I was with Willie I never had a class lesson, it was always one on one. On odd occasions he would bring in three of his other dancers to go through the Reel movements and steps. For music he played a set of miniature pipes and was able to shout instructions while playing the dance tunes and still maintaining pressure in the pipe bag, One of Willie's other boy dancers at that time was Ian Macdonald and Ian kept up that tradition of playing while instructing, in his own classes over later years. Ian, of course, played and was eventually in charge of the Pipers for dancing at Cowal Gathering and his knowledge of the dancing side of music made him one of the best dancing pipers ever. His selection of tunes and his timing were a great benefit to the dancers, allowing them to perform at their very best in what was, after all, the most important and prestigious Championships of the year. Ian, a former serving Black Watch Piper, was following in the tradition of other great Pipe Majors who were also trained dancers, such as Big Angus MacDonald of the Scots Guards, Wee Donald Macleod of the Seaforths and Donald Maclean of Lewis.

Willie used to set me homework tests to make sure I knew the whys and wherefores of the steps and positions and to reinforce his weekly instructions and corrections.

> **Master Billy Forsyth: Bridge of Allen**
>
> | Question (Fling) | Answer |
> |---|---|
> | 1. What do you consider the most important position in Fling? | 1st Position. ✓ |
> | 2. What position is used most in all Highland Dances? | 1st Position. ✓ |
> | 3. What position will your foot be in when you finish the 2nd Step? | 3rd ariel back. ✓ |
> | 4. What position is your foot in at the Toe & heel in 3rd Step? | 3rd Position. ✓ |
> | 5. What position will your foot at the back be in when Rocking in 4th Step? | 3rd Position back. ✓ |
> | 6. What position will your foot be in at the counts 1 and 3 in 5th Step? | 4th Position ✓ |
> | 7. What position will your foot be in at the finish of the 6th Step? | 3rd pos ✓ |
> | 8. What position will your foot be in when it's at the front of leg in 8th Step? | 3rd ariel pos. front. ✓ |
> | 9. What position will your foot be in at the back of leg in the 8th Step? | 3rd ariel pos. back ✓ |
> | 10. What do you consider the most attractive position? | 4th ariel pos. ✓ (and 2nd Position) |
> | 11. What Steps in the Fling do you put both hands up at? | 2nd step, 4th step, 5th step. ✓ |
> | 12. What is deportment? | Holding shoulders back, walking on and off the stage, dancing. ✓ |
>
> 12/12.

I was rarely 100% with the answers, but it kept me on my toes (figuratively as well as practically).

I continued to compete and win prizes and quite a number of Trophies, although at that time there were few Championships, or should I say there were many so-called 'Championships' but few rules on who could run them or how they did so. This was the era before the SOBHD gathered strength and managed to lay down basic standards for adjudicating and organising big events. Most competitions were Open to all within the age groups although there were some events restricted to dancers from a set area. There were certainly no 'Pre-Premier' competitions (Beginner,

Novice, or Intermediate as are available now) though in the smaller hall competitions the Organiser might offer a Beginner event or a 'Consolation' dance for non-prize-winners.

I am the boy on the left in this Fife Press photo 1951.

I soaked up Willie's instructions and tried hard to put them into practice. I was particularly good at the Hornpipe and Irish Jig, where a lot of freedom was given to characterisation. There was a period when I would win virtually every Hornpipe event I entered, but with the Jig I was up against some very strong competitors, particularly Wilma Tolmie from Dundee and Margaret Meldrum from Kirkcaldy, both great friends for many years. Margaret's daughter Gillian Greig went on to win a World Championship and Wilma's family Gareth, Deryck and Ailsa Mitchelson all won many Championships including multiple World Championships.

In 1953 I was overjoyed to win the Scottish Boys Championship for the first time in the Music Hall, Edinburgh at the International Festival of Dancing. As I was only 12 and competing against boys up to 15 years old it was a great victory. I went on to win a further two Scottish Boys Championships.

It was probably my best year to date as I added a Coronation Cup, the Airth Shield and Aboyne's Davidson Quaich to my trophy list.

During those years the family travelled far and wide across Scotland and were introduced by Willie to friends of his in different parts of the country, including on the Road to the Isles. We became great friends of the Macdonald family in Arisaig and through them competed at Lochaber, Glenfinnan, Arisaig and Morar Highland Games. We also managed to reach the Skye Gathering in Portree but found on arrival that there was no Juvenile competition and I had to dance in the 'Open' section against the adult dancers. Not easy when you are up against the likes of James L. Mackenzie, a three times World Champion.

Further south on the West coast a favourite Highland Games was held on the hill overlooking Tobermory Bay on the Isle of Mull. It was a bit disconcerting to begin with, as at that time Gaelic was spoken by most of the islanders, and amongst the audience on the side of the hill Mum & Dad couldn't understand a word they were saying.

For Aboyne and Braemar, because they were held mid-week, Mum and I would generally get the late- night bus from Stirling to Aberdeen, have breakfast in the wee café just off the harbour, used mostly it seemed by fishermen and overnight workers, then took the next bus from Aberdeen to Aboyne in time for the morning events at the Games. Overnight in Aboyne then on to Braemar by bus then finally, after the Gathering there, a bus down the Devil's Elbow Road to Blairgowrie, Perth and home.

6
I was a Voracious Reader of Everything

As a child and young adult I was a voracious reader of anything and everything from factual Sport and Current Affairs to all kind of general children's books.

I particularly liked the weekly Boys Story magazines which covered adventure and activities. They were exciting and involved mainly teenagers and young adults doing all the things boys dream about.

'The Tough of the Track' Alf Tupper in 'The Rover', who beat everyone from 100 yards to One Mile, was a real hero and could turn his hand to other sports such as football or rugby because he was faster than anyone else. He was a real working-class hero as his diet seemed to consist mainly of fish suppers. 'Wilson, the Wonder Athlete' did the same job for 'The Wizard'.

The other story magazine I remember was 'The Hotspur' with similar stories of daring do, including the usual boy-wonder who created ingenious machines, the young soldier or flying ace who won the war on his own and of course the British intelligence officer who tracks down and sorts out those dratted foreigners.

They were text magazines with usually a two-page story or more for each character featured. Although I didn't realise it at the time all were published by the D C Thomson Press in Dundee who, of course, also published 'The Sunday Post', home of 'The Broons' and 'Oor Wullie' strip cartoons which just couldn't be missed. So much so that every Christmas stocking had to include one or other of their 'Annuals' {they were printed every second year) or Christmas wasn't complete.

I used the local and school library a lot and after starting Highland lessons with Willie Cuthbertson in Glasgow I could read a full hardback on the bus before reaching Cumbernauld on the way back.

The timetable was: catch the Glasgow bus coming from Crieff about ten minutes to six at the bus stop outside the Old Mill in Bridge of Allan; arrive at the Glasgow bus stop, first of all at WD & HO Wills factory (for Clayton Terrace) then later opposite the park gates on Alexandra Parade in Glasgow (for Aitken Street) just after seven o'clock: dance lesson until half past eight; catch the Crieff bus at the park gates around twenty to nine: arrive back outside 'The Bridge Inn' around ten fifteen. I suppose the bus would be at the old Cumbernauld Village around twenty-five past nine so maybe around two hours or less to read a full library book.

Those books were mainly adventure and sports stories but I know included some Denis Wheatley novels about black magic and the occult which I eventually had to abandon as they were just a bit too realistic for someone of that age. If you have read any Denis Wheatley, you will know what I mean.

I have read a couple of the 'Famous Five' books by Enid Blyton but they just were not my scene.

I preferred mystery stories where I could try to outwit the author by working out 'who dunnit' before I reached the final chapter. Probably this is why I still enjoy the TV series of that type from Midsomer Murders, Death in Paradise and Vera to (going back a bit) Perry Mason courtroom dramas, Colombo and Kojak.

7
My Best Friend growing up

When we moved to the new house in Cawder Gardens there were lots of young couples with kids also moving into the street.

There were a few new bungalow style houses at the top of Cawder Road where their gardens at the rear backed on to Cawder Gardens, and which also had similar age kids. The Macfarlane family lived in one of them. They had three kids, Ian who was about my age plus twins Ronnie and Betty who were about Andrea's age.

Ian had a medical problem (referred to generally as a hole in the heart) and consequently had spent a lot of time in hospital.

Ian had similar interests to myself, football, athletics, photography, music, and we got on well together. We followed the Commonwealth and Olympic Games events avidly and the Scottish Football results. We covered lots of different subjects as readers but didn't have special favourites.

We were not very similar physically though. I had always played a lot of football, not in a formal team but in the primary school playground and on our own football pitch in the middle of Cawder Gardens against the kids around Cawder Road and Square or sometimes the kids around Cornton Crescent whom we knew through our Primary and early Secondary school years. Ian could hardly run without getting out of breath and was a useless Goalkeeper but tried his best.

After reading the story of the famous Scotland Football team of 1928 which beat England 5 - 1 at Wembley and became known as 'The Wee Blue Devils', as most were very small and the five forwards were all under 5 ft 7 ins, I decided to form my own Blue Devils team and, with the help of a potato cut-out (old school technology), a badge including a very solid bug-eyed Devil complete with horns was duly stamped on a blue ink pad and then transferred onto our 'team shirts'.

The team didn't win too often because the 'Square' and the 'Cornton' kids were better but it was good fun while it lasted.

We even had a 'Blue Devils' athletics meeting, running round the oval that was Cawder Gardens.

Cawder Gardens oval (looking from No. 23) 1953 - Billy & Ian

Because I was a highland dancer, when it came to 'guising' time at Halloween, none of your American trick or treat stuff here in Scotland, I was way ahead of the game. A very profitable few nights were held dancing for the neighbours and some relatives and friends who lived nearby. At that time, it wasn't all sweets and stuff. Disguises were put on and some make-up (usually soot) then after the performance money was exchanged, with juice and even scones or biscuits.

The trouble was what could Ian do to justify his bounty? His usual statement, until forced into reciting a poem, was "I'm his manager and I just take 10% of his earnings".

We experimented with developing and printing our own photos, in black and white, of course, and talked about who was in the Pop Charts and would sell thousands of vinyl records (45 rpm).

We were not quite at the long-playing album (33 rpm) time yet, but long past the old 78 rpm solid disks.

In our mid-teens we bought all the equipment and chemicals needed to develop and print photographs, including a big Enlarger, and blacked out the kitchen in my house or Ian's house as our photo lab, complete with red bulb replacements to ensure we could both see and work 'in the dark'.

When I was visiting Fort William for the games, I took a portrait of Jeanette Millar, one of the Arisaig dancers, and we subsequently developed and printed it back in Bridge of Allan.

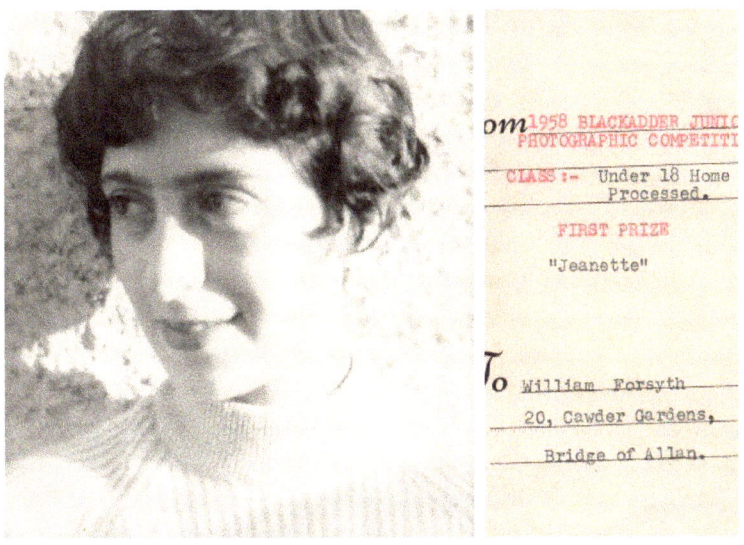

It turned out well and I decided to enlarge it and enter it in a competition run by Blackadders, a Camera shop, in Glasgow. To my surprise it won First Prize.

The judge's comments included praise for the composition and contrasts but suggested if I do it again that I avoid cutting the corners of the photo when mounting it on the backboard. What he didn't know was that the only way we could get the semi-gloss photopaper to lie flat for the enlargement under the heat of its lamp was to use drawing pins to hold it in place. The pinholes and circular outlines then showed up on the finished print so we neatly cut a small triangle off the corners to solve the problem. Needs Must!

As an older teenager, and as a twenty-year-old with a driving licence Ian and I managed quite a few trips around the country. When I eventually bought my first car, actually an A35 van, we stuck a tent and some sleeping bags in the back and set off to the Highland Games and later to Championships further afield in England, including Northumberland, Somerset and London.

During July's traditional holiday period, 'The Glasgow Fair Fortnight', (which starts the first Monday after the second Tuesday – honest) we would tour the country:

Airth on Saturday, Burntisland on the Monday, Inveraray on Tuesday, Luss (Loch Lomond) on Wednesday, up to Oban then over to Tobermory on Mull on Thursday, back to the mainland for Thornton in Fife on Friday then Lochearnhead on Saturday.

If the weather was bad and we didn't fancy the tent we slept in the van or in the Games marquees which were always up and completed the day before the Games.

Hygiene was not a problem as there were many hotels and restaurants or roadhouses which encouraged you to enjoy meals and drinks and all of them had substantial toilets. Discreet coverage of a washbag, morning or night time, enabled hot water shaving and washing and if a campsite had a shower in the toilet block so much the better. No, we didn't normally use campsites but if you 'wild camped' along the road a bit, facilities could usually be just a short walk away.

One famous trip took us for a couple of nights to the Scottish Borders, where Ian had a girlfriend, then on to Newcastle for a couple of nights with dancing friends of mine, then down the A1 (long before it was a dual carriageway) and a couple of nights in Nottingham, (to be followed later by many more nights in Nottingham for obvious reasons). Then a long journey to Butlins

Camp at Minehead in Somerset where I was due to compete (and win) in the West of England Championships sponsored by and held in Billy Butlins vast Holiday Park.

Yes, it was just like the Hi-de-Hi show on TV years ago. Redcoats everywhere, on day-time duty for sports and activities, then taking over the theatre and ballrooms at night for stage shows and dance competitions. It was a great training ground for the actors, musicians, dancers and comedians of the next TV generation of thespians.

Janet Pilling, Ruth Voss, Ian, Mum, the Groom & Bride, Mr. & Mrs. Metheringham, Pat & Andrea

After the US/Canada tours period, Ian and I did not see each other as often but it was to Ian I turned when I sought a Best Man for my wedding to Anne in Nottingham in February 1966.

We were not in touch much on a regular basis after that as my life had become very busy, working and dancing in shows all over the place, and I was surprised after just a couple of years to receive an invitation to Ian's wedding to a girl from Glasgow. At the time I had no idea he was even serious about anyone, but by then I was rarely in the local area other than to sleep and recover from stage and TV shows.

We attended his wedding but sad to say within a few years I heard through his younger brother and sister, who still lived locally, that Ian had died not long after getting married.

8

Mum when I was young

How does anyone describe their own mother? If you think of only the pleasant times and say she was wonderful then you are flattering to deceive. If you think only of problem times and say she was a bit of a dragon then you are being very disloyal and unrealistic. Mum was strict definitely and her standards were high but she could also be great fun and loved social occasions.

My mother came through disturbing life changing events and survived, no, didn't just survive but, with determination and hard work, succeeded in raising her family's and her own standard of living way beyond the normal expectations of the times.

As a young adult she worked firstly as a maid in service in Stirling, then in 1933/34 as a 'clippie' on the buses based at the Balfron depot, and from November 1934 as a machine worker at the cotton mill in Deanston, near Doune.

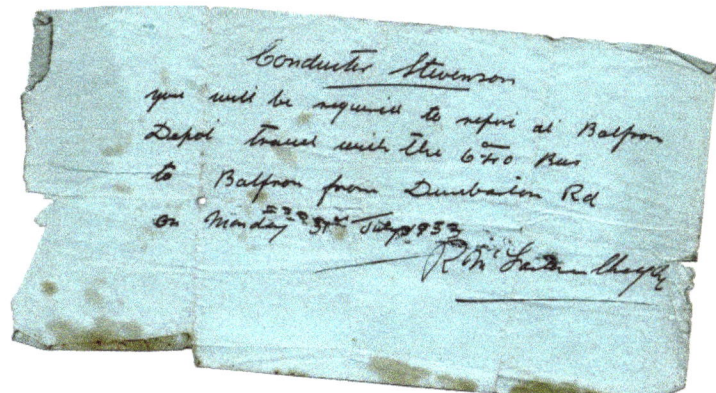

Mum when I was young

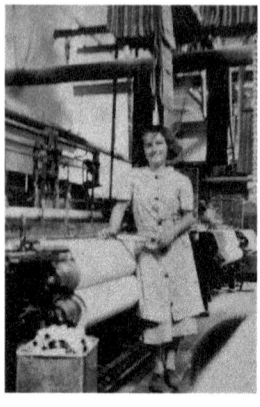 

My Mum and Dad were both keen cyclists and before they were married, members of their local cycling clubs, the Auchterderran Wheelers and Central Scotland Wheelers, as were most of their brothers and sisters.

On 23rd December 1939 they were married in the CSW Club Hall in the old part of St Ninians near the Old Kirk, the official marriage address was 33 Main Street, Stirling.

How they were able to find a white wedding dress for a formal studio photograph I don't know, but once she set her mind to something she almost always made it happen.

In the photo my Uncle John, dad's younger brother, Nan, my Auntie Mary's daughter and Lizzie Jaffray, my mother's cousin.

My Mum spent her entire teens and twenties on bikes. She wrote a diary in an exercise book up until the end of 1937 and noted at the back her cycling mileage day by day. She rode the bike to work, to dances and social events, to the cycling road races and with the CSW club members on their weekend trips around Scotland.

Her mileage is summarised on the back pages:

for 1935 7,025 miles 4,158 for work 2,867 for pleasure

for 1936 8.323 miles 5,392 for work 2,931 for pleasure

for 1937 9,614 miles 6,164 for work, 3,450 for pleasure

Her regular trips with the CSW were to The Trossachs, Loch Lomond, Loch Earn, Dundee, Perth and Killin but some weekend trips took her to Berwick, Dumfries, Dunoon and Carlisle. I remember her saying that, with friends, she did a tour of the north of Scotland in August 1939, ending up at the Cowal Gathering on the last weekend of the month, just as everything changed and war in Europe started.

After the wedding Dad got a job at the Forthbank Rubber Works in Stirling as a neoprene hose maker and Mum joined the A.T.S., the women's equivalent of the Territorial Army, and reported for duty to Stirling Castle, but that didn't last too long as she found she was pregnant with me.

My Dad was called up for National Service and left Mum, like many others, as a single parent until the end of the war in 1945.

During that period my Mum and I lived in a one-bedroom flat (the traditional Scots 'Room and Kitchen) above Tommy Hardie's pub 'The Rising Sun' in New Street, Bridge of Allan.

We had regular visitors from cousins in Fife 'on their holidays' and we took the buses to Fife to visit them in Dundonald, Cardenden and Kirkcaldy.

Mum had always been a keen dancer, Old Tyme, as it was known, a mixture of ballroom round the room sequence dances and Scottish social dances. She had never had formal training so at 3 yrs. old I was sent along to the local Highland teacher for lessons.

Mum when I was young

How Mum managed all this and worked as well I don't know. She had a job in Turnbull's, the local 'Bacon Factory' which was a few minutes away and did babysitting.

When Dad was demobbed and returned home, he was really a stranger to me after six years basically with only my Mum and New Street neighbours, who were mainly women, as the adults around me, hence the impression that she had a very strong influence on me when I was young. It was true, of course. My Dad was always a quiet man and Mum was the organiser supreme and sometimes noisy with it. I was by then no longer a single child, I had a baby sister in the family now and we had moved to a new house at 20 Cawder Gardens, Bridge of Allan.

While Dad worked and sorted out the garden, planted vegetables and laid out paths Mum worked as well as looked after the kids, saved the pennies and made sure we were financially solvent. She was good at that and soon we were the proud owners of a 1936 Morris 8 car which, until it expired (literally) carried us back and forward visiting friends and family all over central Scotland. It was succeeded by a 1938 Morris 10 which had a bit more room inside and a slightly larger engine for my dad to tinker with. As an Army driver Dad was able to keep the cars going until we finally managed to trade up to a new car.

My mother was a regular visitor to Glasgow for shopping and for entertainment and every year until I was 7 yrs., she would take me to 'Jeromes' the photographers in a semi basement studio on Argyll Street for the 'annual photo'. It was usually the train to Glasgow, an afternoon performance of one of the 'big' pantomimes at the Theatre Royal or Alhambra, then tea in a restaurant and finally an evening performance of another show before the train back to Bridge of Allan. It was a real treat.

Mum came up with many ideas for the folks in Cawder Gardens and if necessary, organised the events as well. As a good example, in the Coronation Year 1953, she arranged with the wives and kids to make bunting from scraps of coloured material, cutting them into triangles and sewing them on to strong enough tape to allow it all to be strung from house to house around the houses. Not content with that she organised the men to build a stage on the central grass area to put on a Coronation Carnival with food, music, dancing and a play. As many neighbourhoods around Stirling were also dressing up the streets with bunting for the big day, she then organised a bus so that the kids and families could tour round the area to see what everyone else had done to celebrate the Coronation. She also organised bus trips to Glasgow to see the Christmas Lights and go to the Pantomimes.

Mum was always a saver. having come through a major economic depression and wartime rationing, which lasted into the 1950s, she had to be careful with the finances. She searched all the time for value for money and squirrelled away to the bank account whatever she could.

She brought Andrea and I up to be the same and made sure we had bank accounts from our earliest days. At primary school she would give us money every week to put into our school bank account with the TSB. This was all for a purpose, of course, and was the reason we were able to buy our cars and also take holidays in Europe.

Mum was a very determined woman and her ambitions included buying our own house and taking a post-retirement trip with my dad to visit her relatives in Australia. Once again, she achieved that, although it was soon after we bought the house that my dad took ill and later died.

Despite that major setback she was determined to make that trip on her own and so organised travel and accommodation with friends and family along the route. She left on a ship from Greenock to Montreal in Canada, travelled across Canada by rail to Vancouver, then down the west coast of the USA to Los Angeles. There she boarded a ship which took her via Japan to Melbourne, Australia.

She spent almost three years in Australia, working at different jobs to cover her costs and meeting up with relatives and descendants of her mother's sister's family, who emigrated to Victoria early in the 20th century. She also made many new friends through the Highland Dance community, Scottish clubs and Highland Gatherings, including regular Scottish Country Dance classes and dances.

On her return to Scotland, to see her grandchildren for the first time, she moved into a flat opposite the Old Tolbooth on Broad Street in Stirling, and before long was running a Lunch Club for the pensioners in the 'Top of the Town' from a basement room of the Tolbooth. She continued to find the odd job in Stirling and worked for a while as the telephone base for a local taxi firm in a tiny office next to the Steeple at the top of King Street, and almost under the statue of William Wallace, one of her heroes.

All her life she was a strong supporter of the Scottish National Party and worked as a volunteer in their offices in Stirling during national and local election campaigns. She was a friend to many of the local councillors and SNP MPs having helped many of them on their way up through the ranks in the Party. Nothing was too small for her. Filling envelopes, addressing envelopes, putting on stamps or licking the seal to stick the envelope down, she did it all.

As youngsters the family spent many happy nights at SNP Ceilidhs in Stirling and, quite a few times in Bo'ness as guests of the 'Bo'ness Rebels' group of Nationalists. I still have a copy somewhere of the 'Rebels Ceilidh Songbook' from that era. No wonder Andrea and I loved going to dances and ceilidhs.

Hopefully we have passed that love of dancing on to our own children and grandchildren.

Mum moved eventually to Strathallan Court, the Bield Housing Complex, opposite the football park in Bridge of Allan, where she had her own small flat with a sitting room, bedroom and toilet but had the benefit of a warden on-site and recreational facilities as well. There, with a secure environment behind her, she continued to help with volunteer work for the SNP. It was nothing to her to walk from that flat into Stirling to the latest SNP office/shop to spend the day helping out, and then walking all the way back home again.

This photograph was taken at an SNP Bannockburn Day Rally in Kings Park, Stirling. Although it's not seen in the photo there was a very large Saltire flying from that cane.

Mum when I was young

9

School Days

I started at Bridge of Allan Primary School, in the old building at the bottom of Union Street, in 1946.

The class included all the local kids from the railway station area through to Grahams Farm on the other side of the village and including Cornton Road and Cornton Crescent as far as the level crossing. There was a small Primary School at Lecropt overlooking the station but as the Perthshire County boundary at the time was along the rail line, that school only took in the kids from the farms on the carse and Keir estate.

This photo was taken in autumn 1947 of the BofA Primary 2 class with our teacher Miss Lomax.

I am in the front row on the left.

School Days

You can tell from the clothing it was immediately post-war when everything was make-do and mend. I became very good at darning the holes in my socks and ripping down old jumpers etc. to provide wool for Mum to knit new ones.

We had a very large playground in front of the school which was fairly flat, the only break a drainage channel halfway across the tarmac, and this became our football pitch before assembly, at break times and at lunchtimes. The boys seemed to spend their whole primary school days playing football on that pitch. There was a school hall which ran along the front of the school building and which was used for everything from gym classes to medical exams and vaccinations.

School itself was fairly straightforward and I seem to have done reasonably well through the various classes. In Primary 6 when all the exams had finished, I ended up as a runner-up to the Dux Medalist.

Left to right—Dux, Moir Fotheringham; runners-up (equal)—Billy Forsyth, Senga Scott, Gordon Bryce.

We didn't have the luxury of long-distance trips at school but we did manage a two week stay at Dounans Camp just outside Aberfoyle, school but on an outdoor basis. Dormitory accommodation, dinner hall meals and, for most of us, looking after ourselves, washing, dressing etc. for the very first time away from home. Apart from some regular classroom lessons we spent a lot of time out and around the Aberfoyle area, walking up the Duke's Pass and over the hill to view Loch Drunkie, Loch Achray and Loch Venachar. We did a lot of walking in the regular crocodile formation around the area.

We visited the site of Dounans Camp recently and lo and behold it still exists as part of the Scottish Outdoor Education Centres and really looks little different from 70 years ago.

The High School of Stirling

The traditional first day photo, Andrea to BofA Primary and Billy to High School of Stirling

It was drummed into us from day 1 that it was the High School of Stirling, 'The School on the Rock', never Stirling High. We had many famous former pupils including Muir Mathieson, the Composer of the music for many screen movies and John Grierson, the so-called 'Father of the Documentary Film'. The school even had its own night telescope at the top of the main tower.

School Days

At High School I took French and Latin in addition to English, Maths, Geography and History, resulting in poor French language skills and a smattering of knowledge about Caesar's Gaelic Wars, which was the standard basic Latin text. I did excel at Geography and was passable in History

Into 4th year and a switch to Economics, Mercantile Law and Accounts was much more successful and led me towards an eventual life in finance.

10
Childhood Toys

Toys were a precious asset back in the early 1940s. I don't recall many toys and the ones I do remember are outdoor ones. My three-wheeled trike and my little car with its small steering wheel linked through the various metal rods to the front wheels, and the hinged pedals linked with rods to the back wheels which, with a lot of effort, pushed the car forward. As you will understand photos are far and few from that era, so the ones I do have tend to be taken during fund-raising events.

Here is a photo taken in 1947 with my sister Andrea and a doll called Georgina. From the background it must have been taken at the front door of the flat in New Street, Bridge of Allan.

Childhood Toys

Georgina was made from a hard Bakelite material (which was an early form of plastic) and had moveable arms and legs. In this photo it looks like she was dressed in some of Andrea's baby tops and leggings. I remember this doll and its name because it was my toy for my first few years and I was very attached to it. I imagine that at some time later it was cracked and broken and eventually discarded as Bakelite was not a great material and very brittle.

When my dad was demobbed and we moved to Cawder Gardens, I remember him producing all sorts of toys from chunks of wood. Cars, trains, lorries etc. I must have been into transport then.

Over my early school years every year at Christmas I received one 'big' toy and for a long time it was a Meccano Set. It comprised a whole series of punched-out metal strips in varying lengths with flat squared or rectangular pieces also punched out round the sides. With tiny nuts and bolts and metal wheels with rubber 'tyres' it was possible to build all sorts of constructions from cars and diggers and cranes to garages, houses and large buildings.

Meccano was sold in boxed 'sets' numbered from 00 upwards and as the set numbers grew so did the size and complexity of the items in them. They expanded to include small electric motors and cylinders so that the range of builds became enormous. I suppose it was the precursor to the Lego system which does much the same now for kids (and adults).

Dancing Through Life

Can't find a boxed set of my era so here is the modern version which are sold as individual projects.

In later years I was into music and photography hence my old Dansette record player, my Grundig battery portable tape recorder (which varied in speed), and the various cameras and all the equipment required to develop, print and enlarge the photos taken.

I also had a crystal radio in a white Bakelite case with a long length of wire which acted as the aerial. If you ask anyone of my era about pop music the first thing they will probably talk about is Radio Luxembourg which existed long before Pirate Radio became a craze in the UK.

During my teen-age years like many local kids I built, and raced along the nearby roads, four-wheel go-carts made from old pram wheels, similar to the ones Oor Wullie used in the weekly Sunday Post cartoon strips.

Childhood Toys

Our favourite run was down the pavement (most of the time) of the main road, from the bridge over the railway to the beginning of the narrow path to the Old Bridge, opposite the Bridge Inn. At that time this was the main north road from the central belt to Perth, Aberdeen and Inverness so fairly busy.

While tearing down the pavement you just hoped nobody came out of the driveways which ran off the Station Brae. We had no brakes. Thank goodness at that time there were no cars in those driveways.

With thanks as always to DC Thomson for my childhood years of their fabulous stories and cartoons.

11
My Dad when I was Young

My Dad was a very quiet man, thoughtful and well read, with many interests from football to opera, and was a good singer, as were most of his sisters and his brother. He grew up in the Fife mining village of Bowhill and, as always at that time, was expected to become a Coal Miner as were his friends and his father and grandfather.

He was given the opportunity to go to the Fife Mining School in Cowdenbeath to study engineering but being the oldest son in the family it was up to him to bring wages into the house so did not go there.

He was a member of the local Auchterderran Wheelers Cycling Club and with the rest of his family spent a lot of time on a bike. It

My Dad when I was Young

was through that club that he met my Mum and moved through to Stirling where he became a hosemaker with the Forthvale Rubber Works at the junction of Cornton Road with Causewayhead Road (the site is now a university flats complex called Charles Forte Court). He was called up for Military Service and joined the Royal Signals at Catterick Camp in the north of England.

749 Squad R.Signals 1942 (Sgt. Stenning)

He was given a licence to drive military vehicles and eventually was posted to serve in North Africa, then Sicily and Italy, following the infantry (including the Scottish 51st Highland Division) with the communications units.

He sent many postcards when he was in Italy as he was based for a long time in Naples and he also purchased and managed to send back home a small, one octave, piano accordion which although tiny was playable and a favourite toy of mine. He had the opportunity to visit the famous San Carlo Opera Theatre in Naples, the oldest opera house in the world, and sent home some of the programmes from there.

One of my most vivid memories was of him taking me to see the film 'The Great Caruso' at the old Regal Cinema in Stirling when I was about ten or eleven.

Many, many years later I visited Naples for a European Youth Hostels Conference on Training and Development and was able to see a performance in the San Carlo. Although it was out of season for Opera, I saw the San Carlo Ballet Company perform Cinderella in an almost full theatre.

The Theatre itself was overpowering in its grandeur and I really did feel as if I had been transported back to the early 1800s. No seat in the stalls for me on this special visit, but a box in one of the Grand Circles which swept right round the interior of the building.

It was very strange to think that around 60 years earlier, towards the end of the war in Italy, my dad, with some of his military colleagues, would have been sitting in that same theatre watching some of the greatest opera singers of their time. I know my dad's favourites were Il Pagliacci and Aida but it seems he saw many shows there.

Dad was given his military release papers in September 1945 and came home to Bridge of Allan where Mum had managed to let a small flat from Tommy Hardy, a local publican, who ran The Rising Sun.

My Dad when I was Young

It was a strange feeling to have a man in the flat, someone I had only seen in photos and from the postcards received during the war years. He was a very quiet man so after a while it started to feel normal, but it still took time for me to accept him.

When Andrea arrived and we moved to a new house in Cawder Gardens, it seemed we became a new family amongst other new families starting life again after all the problems of wartime.

Dad was a worker and started laying out the gardens at the front and back of our house and eventually forming a driveway from the pavement up the side of the house to the wooden garage he had built. It backed onto the wire fence to the cornfield which separated us from the railway embankment. He planted flowers and lots of vegetables in the large back garden and also managed to rent a 'plot' (an allotment) alongside Cornton Road which furnished even more fresh veg. We always had lots of carrots, potatoes and lettuce from his efforts.

All the time he worked at the Rubber Works he cycled there and back every day. One strange thing I remember from then, was that he always dismounted the bike by swinging his right leg over the handlebars onto the ground. Everyone else I knew would swing their leg over the saddle.

Dad had been given a Military Driving Licence when he joined the Army but I never knew whether he had to pass a driving test, either then or when he became a civilian again.

He had a habit when driving of holding the steering wheel with his right hand while sitting his left hand on his left thigh. For some reason I have found myself doing the same thing when I drive.

At family gatherings in the evening whether in Fife or around Stirling with my Mum's brothers and sister, there were always a few songs with Dad and others asked to sing their favourites. Dads included 'Mary of Argyll', 'One Full Bumper More' and at Hogmanay 'A Guid New Year'.

Dad liked a dram but never to excess, but that was probably as much to do with the cost as anything else. I don't believe the way our later generations spend money without thinking of the consequences. We had to earn every penny the hard way by working for it so spending was done on an 'as necessary' basis not 'as wanted' or 'as seen on TV' or in a magazine.

One of his favourite pastimes was working out puzzles and he and I spent ages doing one which was a daily spot in one of the newspapers. It asked you to work out the names of places in Scotland based on cryptic clues and some of the clues were very cryptic. G was often represented as half a horse ??, and I remember I being for Novello?? Work them out for yourselves.

We used similar word games as fundraisers for the Tattoo Ceilidh Dancers in the 1990s – 2000s.

Dad was a smoker all his life. After leaving the forces he would buy 10 Woodbine at a time but he later moved to Players. He never smoked to excess but he enjoyed a cigarette with a mug of tea.

Our house No. 20 is the first house on the right in this picture

He was very practical and would join with the other parents in Cawder Gardens to decorate the houses or build a stage or whatever, to make sure the kids all had a good time at Celebrations. For the 1953 Coronation while Mum and other wives cut up material and sewed pennants onto string/tape, Dad was part of the installation squad attaching the bunting to windows and lampposts around the Cawder Gardens Arena making sure everyone was included.

Photo from late 50s

Although Mum learned to drive in her late 40s, during my school years it was always Dad who drove us when we travelled around. We had any number of cars over the years, starting off with real old pre-war bangers, but gradually worked our way up to our first new Car an Austin A30, which was followed by the next version, the A35, and then the Farina designed A40, in which we travelled to the continent, visiting France, Italy, Austria, Germany Belgium and the Netherlands, all with either our tent in the back or towing the trailer which folded out and up to form a two-bedroom tent with its own awning and built-in kitchen. It didn't seem to matter whether we drove on the right or the left Dad just coped with the driving and the signposts.

While I duly had driving lessons and eventually passed my driving test, it was mainly because Mum and Dad took me out driving and gave me a good base of knowledge about road courtesy and safety, that I was also able to negotiate driving in different countries and on the opposite side of the road.

I'm sure the road sense they had from years and years of cycling was transferred to me and the fact that I had grown up in a car-using environment meant that I already had some of the skills necessary to be a competent driver.

There have never been very many photos of my dad because he was generally the one who took the photos until my 'photography' interest in my mid to late teens.

The last decent photo of my dad was taken at my 21st Birthday Party in October 1961 in the Masonic Hall, Bridge of Allan. He was there all dressed up in a dark suit with a bow tie. At that time, we didn't know that a few months later things would change dramatically when he took ill.

He thoroughly enjoyed the evening in the company of about 60 friends and relations, all having a great time singing and dancing the night away, thanks to a Scottish Dance Band led by Joe Burke our Caledonia Tour Accordionist at one end of the hall, and a Rock Band at the other end of the hall, courtesy of our young downstairs neighbour at that time, who was originally from North Wales, and had brought his 'Beatles' style guitar band up for the occasion.

A few years after those photos were taken Dad was diagnosed with a rare muscle wasting disease which eventually meant he couldn't use his arms or hands properly. He was confined to sitting in chairs and unable to go out much. He still liked a cigarette however so we fixed up a frame to hold his cigarette and if we lit it, he could move enough to get a few puffs on his own.

Dad was eventually taken into hospital as he needed 24-hour care and died in December 1965 just 2 months before I was due to be married in February 1966

12

My Working Life

My working life has been varied, of that there is no doubt, and I don't think my parents, or even myself, could have forecast any of the various roles I have played over these many years.

After leaving school in 1958, encouraged by my Mum and Dad (who funded my costs) I was apprenticed to a firm of accountants in the centre of Glasgow (very Victorian) at the princely wage of 80 pounds per annum, paid at a rate of six pounds thirteen shillings and four pence per month.

The attraction, apparently, was that after five years, with hard work, and after passing various exams, I should become a Member of the Institute of Chartered Accountants of Scotland and thereafter the world would rush to hire me at extraordinary salary levels.

As you will have guessed things didn't work out quite as my Mum and Dad envisaged.

I had always been good with the Arithmetic aspect of maths, though not so great with Trigonometry or Algebra. I had taken a commercial based course in senior High School including Economics, Bookkeeping and Mercantile History and Law, which had given me a taster of financial matters.

We lived only two minutes from the station so it was a daily commute from Bridge of Allan to Glasgow, on a steam train of course. Three of the other travellers from Stirling were also accountancy students so there were many discussions on our office experiences and on exam subjects during the journey.

Apart from evening classes twice a week during the winter at the Institute's HQ in St Vincent Street, the major source of knowledge was sourced from working with the senior students and qualified members of the firms' staff either on Audit visits to client company's premises or on clients' tax administration matters in the office. Clients ranged from Local Authorities like Renfrewshire and Argyll County Councils to the SSEB (the South of Scotland Electricity Board) and the Bridge of Weir Leather Company, suppliers to such as Rolls Royce Motors.

As junior assistants our main duties were of the 'bump and tick' variety. Most basic audit work at that time comprised of checking a selection of transactions from each monthly list against the original invoice/voucher/authorisation by applying an audit stamp to the voucher and a tick against the line item on the (usually) computer generated summary, hence the 'bump and tick' expression. Although completely boring work, which rarely produced major errors, it was more likely to highlight where a cost may have been charged to the wrong cost centre than anything else. The experience however gave me an insight into how firms and public bodies structured their financial administration and how management oversight was organised.

To be with a qualified accountant walking into those companies also taught us very quickly that a high standard of behaviour was required at all times as we were usually dealing with the Directors and Senior Managers of the companies. At the SSEB offices we had lunch in the staff canteen but at the Bridge of Weir Leatherworks we were invited to lunch in the Directors' Dining Room which was a formal affair.

It was in the Dunoon offices of Argyll County Council that I first met and spoke with a number of the Board members of Cowal Gathering as some of them were senior Council Officers.

The first year or so of apprenticeship went well if a bit unnerving at times, and the required exams were duly passed, however things were about to change after I received an offer that was difficult to refuse.

The week after the 1960 Cowal Gathering I received a call from Andrew Macpherson, leader of the group 'Caledonia', asking if I would join his group as lead dancer on a tour of the United States and Canada.

After I got over the immediate shock, I asked for more information and was told the contracted dancer had pulled out at the last minute and he was seeking a replacement. He had already spoken to Flora Stuart Grubb, an Australian dancer whom I knew, who was competing in Scotland that summer, and she had suggested that he phone me. Flora had postponed her return to Australia in order to join the group. There were 18 members of the group which was based on The Andrew Macpherson Chorale, plus a pianist, piper, accordionist and myself and Flora. The tour was over a period of five months and due to depart in four weeks.

Having discussed everything with family and friends and decided that it was an opportunity not to be missed I approached my employers and, with conditions, was given a leave of absence by them.

The following weeks were frantic - rehearsals for a show which would run to almost two hours; measurements and fittings for a new full kilt outfit, cut for me to be able to dance easily, and organizing clothing, medical vaccinations and travel documentation for the tour.

We managed it all but everything was a rush.

Due to a technical problem at Glasgow Renfrew Airport, we were delayed 24 hours on departure, eventually rebooked on a British Airways flight from Prestwick Airport the following day, and on my 20th birthday, and purely by chance, I was handed a first-class boarding pass. Flying first class to New York, what a birthday present.

The tour ended at the beginning of February 1961 and after a short break I went back to the office.

Into Showbusiness full-time

The Caledonia Show tour was very successful and on our return to Scotland an offer was made by the American Booking Agency for a second tour of USA and Canada the following winter.

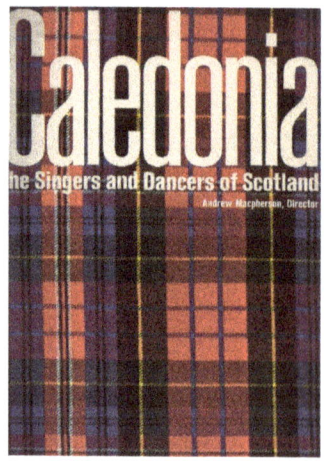

It would be impossible to continue in accountancy if I intended to go on the second tour so a decision had to be made. I suppose it was inevitable that I signed a contract for a further USA & Canada tour.

The choreographer for the first tour was Bruce McClure who was at the time the Dance Director at Scottish Television. Having committed to 'Caledonia' I was asked to join the dance group organised by Bruce for the autumn series of STV's Scottish show 'Jigtime'.

I now had an Agent, Ross Bowie, who produced stage shows and arranged tours at home and abroad for many Scottish artistes. When STV's Hogmanay Show, networked throughout the UK, was broadcast live from the Olympia Ballroom in East Kilbride and included the Andrew Macpherson Chorale, myself and Margaret Gordon were the featured dancers.

On completion of the 1962 American Tour Margaret and I were booked by Ross Bowie as a double act for the annual Summer Show at the Cragburn Pavilion in Gourock, then for various one-off performances in Theatres around Scotland.

We were booked again for the STV Hogmanay Show that winter and after the sudden death of Bruce McClure I was named Dance Director. With many technical problems during rehearsals and the programme running short I was asked to increase the number of dances being performed. It was broadcast to the STV region at 11.30 pm then went on to the UK network at 11.45pm. It ended up as a Dance Ceilidh with other acts breaking up the dance programme.

Meantime the usual Burns Night, St Andrews Night and Hogmanay TV shows came up and a new STV series was produced for which I continued to be Dance Director.

However, opportunities to perform, in general, were becoming fewer and I went back to combining a regular job with semi-pro dancing in shows and theatres with such as Rikki Fulton, Jack Milroy, Jimmy Logan, Kenneth McKellar, the Alexander Brothers, Anne and Laura Brand, Jim Macleod's Band and other Scottish artistes.

I went back into office administration with a job at Forthvale Rubber Works, where my dad had worked many years before.

From there I moved to the NCB offices in Alloa then, thanks to a connection of my cousin, who worked at the BMC Truck and Tractor plant in Bathgate, I ended up there as cost control officer for the Tractor plant.

While at BMC I saw an advert for a position in the finance department of Donaldson Brothers (Donbros Knitwear) in Alloa and moved there in 1966. It was a well-known brand name in the UK knitwear trade.

Immediately on my arrival the Managing Director asked me to review the raw material control and handling systems which at the time, apparently, produced a lot of excess material, in particular small lots of dyed knitting yarn. After presenting my recommendations, he asked me to take over full responsibility for the purchase, receipt, storage and distribution to the knitting machines of the raw materials and the efficient cost control of them.

During my time there the company was taken over twice, first by Pasolds, a childrenswear manufacturer, then by Coats Patons, a major company in the textile industry who were well known in Alloa through Patons and Baldwins, knitting yarn producers, a major employer in the town at that time.

I spent nine years with Donbros and during the last year was asked to take over the position of Purchasing Officer for the firm after the retiral of the then incumbent. I was disappointed that the company made no attempt to retain me when I later handed in my notice but all became clear when later that week an announcement was made that Coats Patons Group had decided to close the site and incorporate the production into various other sites, mainly outside Scotland.

My next-door neighbour in Ogilvie Place, Bridge of Allan, worked part-time in the Stirling headquarters of the Scottish Youth Hostels Association. In 1975 she said joking, that the accountant had left to travel overseas and the job would suit me as, in her opinion, he did very little. Was that a dig at him or me?

After some thought, for I was settled with Donbros, I decided to phone the General Secretary to ask about the position. He said he was very busy but would see me for a short discussion at 8.30 am one morning before the Office opened for the day.

I duly arrived had a pot of tea with him and a general chat about the operation of SYHA, which was much bigger than I had expected. SYHA was the biggest provider of accommodation in the whole of Scotland, with over 5000 beds spread over almost 100 properties from the far north to the southern border with England. I finally left the building about 11 am, so much for a quick chat.

We found we had a lot in common in our backgrounds despite an age difference of about 25 years, he as a walker, cyclist and hosteller and my family as cyclists and campers. It seemed that my finance background with cost control, plus young family, wife as a nurse and involvement with highland dancing also fitted into his idea of who might fit the bill. By the time I left his office we had struck up a good relationship. He did not have carte blanche to hire the new person on his own and I duly went through a series of interviews with the Chairman and Finance Convenor of the Association.

In October 1975 I finally started at the Glebe Crescent, Stirling headquarters as Finance Officer. Over the years my role developed to assist with investigation and implementation of computerised systems, first of all moving from electric typewriters to word processors and eventually financial control systems, for which an area had to be sectioned off with air conditioning to contain the new computer system. We then set up an SYHA website and ultimately devised and installed an online SYHA hostel bed booking system, the first of any Youth Hostel organisation worldwide. We demonstrated it to the world at an International Conference in New York by dialing in to the Stirling Computer system from a laptop and making a booking at one of our Youth Hostels.

I thoroughly enjoyed my time with SYHA, the work was varied and I was able to contribute in a number of different areas, not just finance but also, for example in Marketing. While travelling in different parts of the world for dancing and judging I would collect and bring back to Scotland some of the advertising materials and styles which were being used there. When the General Secretary who appointed me retired and his deputy took over, I was promoted to Deputy and when eventually he retired, I was made Chief Executive of the organisation.

As Deputy and then CEO I travelled extensively all over Europe and to International Conferences held in India and the United States. Despite an intention to visit all of the Scottish Youth Hostels within a few years of being appointed as Finance Officer in 1975, I still hadn't done so after 25 years in post, reaching only about 80% of them.

Since retiring I have added another three hostels in the North of Scotland to my list of visits but it seems unlikely I'll add to that total any more.

13
Overseas dancing trips back in the day

If you don't count visits to Dunoon, and the islands of Mull and Skye, my first 'Overseas' trip was in 1957 to Douglas on the Isle of Man with the Anchor Mills Pipe Band and a group of dancers organised by Jean Dickson, a dance teacher in Paisley. Eleanor Dickson and Sandy McNidder were two of the other dancers. We flew from the old Renfrew Airport in a big square turbo prop aircraft. I have no memory of why I was in the group other than I had been doing well in competitions and knew the Dickson family.

In May 1958 I was a member of an SOBHD team representing Scotland in Dublin at an Irish Folk Dance and Song Festival. We travelled on the overnight ferry from the Broomielaw in Glasgow. On arrival we performed at various events around Dublin, including at a Military Tattoo in the then new Santry National Stadium, with a number of International Military Bands and Dance Groups.

The team was Marjory Rowan from Edinburgh, Betty Jessiman from Huntly, Alice Stuart from Aberdeen, Marjory Greig from Kirkcaldy, Iain Macdonald from Glasgow, George Seivwright from Aberdeen and myself from Bridge of Allan. The Piper was Lewis Turrell, a New Zealander who spent a year in Scotland competing at all the major Solo competitions. The group was led by Baillie Frank Stewart from the City of Edinburgh Council, who was also the organiser of the Annual International Festival of Dance and the Arts.

Overseas dancing trips back in the day

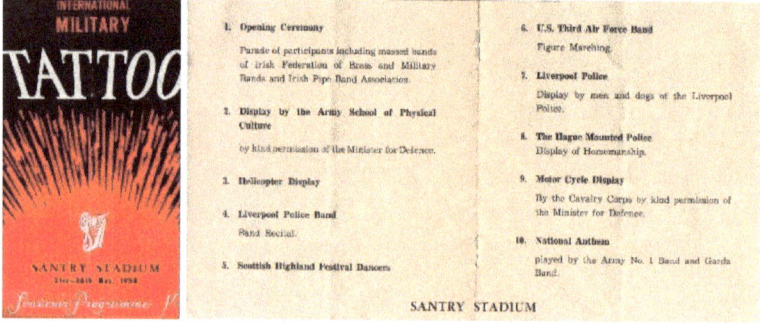

During the trip we visited the usual tourist spots including the Guinness Brewery and Jamesons Distillery, where we were each given a small miniature of their famous Irish Whiskey. One thing I can remember is that, not being a drinker, I tucked the miniature into the top pocket of my tweed highland jacket and forgot about it. On the ferry back to Glasgow the bottle which had a cork seal must have come loose for when I woke in the morning everything smelled of Jamesons best and it appeared as if I had had a good night.

My next Overseas dancing trip was with the 'Caledonia' show as a member of the Andrew Macpherson group which toured the States and Canada twice in 1960/61 and 1962 but the story of those tours could fill a book on their own so I'll leave the full story of that for another day. I can confirm however that spending five months with a group of 18 singers and dancers, roaming all over the USA with side trips into the major Canadian cities, certainly makes you grow up fast. With Flora Grubb from Australia on the first trip, and Margaret Gordon from the north of England on the second tour, as featured lead dancers, we had an absolute ball seeing new places and meeting all sorts of new people in theatres and concert venues which held usually in excess of 2000 seats.

1962 Tour Margaret Gordon and Billy Forsyth MBE

After winning the World Championships and performing in many stage and TV shows my world expanded enormously and led to many more overseas trips.

I have been asked to Adjudicate Championships in Canada, the United States, South Africa and Australia over the years and for a long time became the 'International Voice of Highland Dancing' through hosting and compering major Highland Dance Championships and shows around the world.

I have also particularly enjoyed my visits to Japan and meeting many of the Highland and Scottish Country dancers there. My first visit was with a group organised by David Webster of the Scottish Council for Physical Recreation (SCPR), and himself an organiser of Indoor and Outdoor Highland Gatherings in the UK and Overseas. In 1969 David was organiser and leader of a group sponsored by McVitties Biscuits, who presented a Scottish Highland Gathering in one of the great parks in Tokyo during a British Trade Mission to Japan.

While the experience was amazing and the hospitality quite wonderful, it was never in my mind that I would be interviewed in a TV programme by a Giant Toad. Something new every day.

This visit however resulted in one of the most amazing friendships, which has lasted over many, many years. The Bluebell Club is a Scottish Country Dance Club in Tokyo attached to the RSCDS in Scotland and a demonstration team, all of whom were Japanese, from the club performed at the Highland Games. A number of years afterwards I took a phone call on a Sunday evening which initially sounded strange.

Dancing Through Life

The conversation went like this – (imagine a Japanese accent)

Mr. Forsyth? Yes.

Mr. Billy Forsyth? Yes again

Mr. Billy Forsyth, Highland Dancer? Yes again.

Ah, my name is Marchand, I was a member of Country Dance team at McVitties Games in Tokyo.

I have tried to find you to ask if you would come to Tokyo as our Dance Judge at our Highland Games.

Marchand was in Scotland to attend the RSCDS Annual General Meeting and their Summer School in St Andrews. She was in a rush to go back to Glasgow to return home but had taken the opportunity of a requirement to change trains in Stirling to phone my number she had obtained from someone, and was delighted to finally make contact with me.

Later that year I flew to Tokyo to attend their Highland Games and was surprised to find that the Games Organiser had been a former Stirling University Chaplain, Stuart Picken, who, after marrying a Japanese girl, moved to the Christian University in Tokyo. He still had a house in Dunblane, two miles from my house.

Since that first visit, through the auspices of Marchand and her husband Yukio, I have been to Japan many times and not only judged at their games but have organised trips for the Vale of Atholl Pipe Band, the Simon Howie Dance Band and a singer and dancers for a festival in Kamagari, near Hiroshima.

The Vale and dancers Gregor Bowman, Gillian Greig , Scotland, Anne Milne & Jennifer Lindsay, Canada

When the Atholl Highlanders were invited to a promotion in Japan they asked if I would step in as a dancer for one of their members who was injured and also compere their presentations.

Marchan is on the left in this photo, one of very few I have of her, the others are Bluebell Club dancers

My job was to explain the story of the Atholl Highlanders, to talk about the music and the dances of Scotland and to perform solo and also with the Highlanders in a four-man Argyll Broadswords.

In later years, for six years in a row, with my wife Denise, I took a group of four of my younger Royal Edinburgh Tattoo Dancers to a summer Scottish Festival in Japan which was held in a Swiss Alpine style hotel which had been built as part of the complex for the Winter Olympics in Hakuba, near Nagano.

Of course in the summer the hotel was not busy and Scottish country and highland dancers from all over Japan took the opportunity for a long weekend festival of music and dance. The organisers had asked especially for four of our younger members

who could explain how they came to dance, how they learned the steps and movements of Scotland's traditional dances and could then demonstrate their excellent technical standards for the audience.

Hakuba 2010 in Scottish and Japanese Dress

Apart from the chance to see Japan through the eyes of Japanese people who take part in lots of Scottish dance activities, the girls were able to walk through the centre of Tokyo, eat in typical Japanese Restaurants (plus MacDs and TG Fridays) experience a few nights in a very compact small hotel in Tokyo, and see the real countryside as Habuka was in the western mountains, six driving hours from Tokyo. When asked what they especially wanted to do in Tokyo on their last free day there, all opted for a visit to Tokyo Disneyland, such are our teenagers.

Among many other overseas trips, I visited The Gambia and Senegal in West Africa, Mexico and Ecuador in South America and Puerto Rico in the USA, all as promotional trips with British Caledonian Airways as explained elsewhere.

As a result of meeting a Scottish Country Dance teacher in The Gambia I was also invited to Karachi in Pakistan where Margaret Fell and her husband had moved after he was transferred with his job in pharmaceuticals distribution.

It gave me an opportunity to go up-country, flying to Lahore and travelling by car to Sialkot, where I talked to a local producer of Scottish goods and then on to Peshawar in the far North-West. Margaret warned me that they had an expression within the ex-pat community of 'NQR' translated as 'Not Quite Right' so watch carefully what you have produced here. As it happens Margaret had friends in the Coats Paton companies there who then arranged to have Pipe Banners made locally, of good quality, for the Vale of Atholl Juvenile Pipe Band, as the Hostels Association had agreed to sponsor the youngsters during the SYHA 50th anniversary year.

We did try to venture from Peshawar towards the Afghanistan Border at the Khyber Pass but, a few miles out from the city, the road was blocked by a large group of heavily bearded local men with guns who indicated we should turn back. We did.

We also found out that in the hotel alcohol drink was not readily available however, if you wished to have a beer or two, you could sign a declaration that you absolutely needed alcohol to live, and miraculously a beer would appear. I signed. I couldn't miss out on that. It was too good an opportunity to tell another, just about believable, story to the folks back home.

Does that make me a registered alcoholic?

Incidentally, approaching Peshawar Airport there is a sign which reads 'Guns must be put in your Hold Luggage',

I kid you not.

14

The Stone of Destiny - Any Connection?

T   *he Dean o' Westminster's a funny wee man,*
    He hauds aw the strings o' the state in his hand,
    But wi' aw these fine notions
It bothers him nane,
When some deils ran away wi' his wee magic stane.

From the Bo'ness Rebels Ceilidh Song Book

The date: Christmas Day 1950

The location: Westminster Abbey, London

The students: Ian Hamilton, Gavin Vernon, Alan Stuart and Kay Matheson

The Stone of Scone - the ancient inaugural stone of the Scottish kings - had been taken by the forces of Edward I in 1296. Since then it had been in Westminster Abbey, set under the throne of the English kings. The first Scots royal to sit on it again had been James VI and I at his English coronation in 1603. In the post-war decades Scottish autonomy became an issue. The Scottish Nationalists secured their first MP, Dr Robert McIntyre, in the Motherwell by-election of 1945, while the Scottish Covenant movement of 1949 had called for reform of the constitution of Scotland and for self-government within the UK. In Glasgow a small group of Nationalist students decided to strike a blow for Scottish pride.

The Stone of Destiny - Any Connection?

On Christmas Day 1950 four of them - Ian Hamilton, Kay Matheson, Alan Stuart and Gavin Vernon - decided to repatriate the stone. It was eventually returned to Westminster in time for the Queen to sit on it at her coronation, but the ancient grudge remained. It was only in 1996 that the stone was returned to Scotland.

It's a long way from Westminster Abbey to Bo'ness and I have no means of verifying the following story so I won't even try, however here it is as given to me.

When I was in my early teens, as a family, we attended many social and political events in Stirling and around the local area. The local SNP branch held meetings and dances in a hall upstairs next to Menzies Car Garage and Showroom in Orchard Place, Stirling (now all part of the Thistle Centre).

At those events Mum and Dad met many members from other branches who came to the socials. Andrea and I joined in the dancing and were known to many of the local councillors and branch members, Provost Dr Robert McIntyre (later SNP President) and his wife, Leila, Robert Campbell and his wife, Sandy Milne (at that time single, later married Moira), branch stalwarts Jimmy Lindsay and Iain McIntyre, all were good dancers and regulars wherever there was a function.

At one of those functions we met a group from the Bo'ness Branch who styled themselves "the Bo'ness Rebels", a mix of young and enthusiastic SNP supporters. We were given an invitation to one of their Ceilidhs in Bo'ness. I don't remember the venue but there was a local pub which seemed to be an SNP stronghold and it was probably there. The name 'The Auld Hoose' rings a bell but maybe the owner's name was 'Auld'. At the ceilidh we were asked back to a local house where Grant Shaw, one of the Bo'ness Rebels, lived with his dad and Grannie. Another ceilidh developed there. As the night wore on we were urged to stay so Mum and Dad were allocated a room and I ended up in the box bed built into the kitchen/sitting room wall.

Those ceilidhs were very traditional with many of the group giving a rendition of their favourite Scots songs and just about everyone joining in the Choruses, lots of music and dancing. It was there that I was given a copy of the Bo'ness Rebels Ceilidh Song Book, a booklet of songs written mainly by local scribes, all based on the return of Independence to Scotland and very much in a republican manner.

Scotland hasnae got a King and it hasnae got a Queen,
Ye cannae hae the second Liz when the first yin hasnae been,
Nay Liz the Wan, nae Lilibet the Twa,
Nae Liz will ever dae,
For we'el mak our land Republican in the Scottish Breakaway.

From the Bo'ness Rebels Ceilidh Song Book

Now Grant Shaw, who would have been about 18 to 20 at the time, and his dad, were certainly not involved in the repatriation of The Stone of Scone, or even the hiding of it around Scotland before it was handed over and placed in the area of the High Altar in the ruined Arbroath Abbey three months after being taken, but they certainly were aware of some of the people who were involved. Whether there were some or any of the Bo'ness Rebels helping to move the Stone during that period, who knows, but they certainly enjoyed the pantomime surrounding the search for the Stone and the many false leads the Police were given to locate it. Some of the songs in their Songbook were based on the ramifications of the Repatriation of the Stone and the subsequent newspaper headlines and articles.

We didn't actively keep in touch with the Rebels from Bo'ness but met many of them at Highland Games and SNP events for many years afterwards. Because I was competing at many of the Games, as they knew me, they would seek me out to say hello.

Grant Shaw left home and joined the Merchant Navy. He had already left home before this and become a cabin boy on ships but returned to Bo'ness at times to see the family. I met up with him quite a few times when he was in dock in Glasgow.

The Stone of Destiny - Any Connection?

A few years later he asked me to be his Best Man at his wedding to Doreen in deepest home counties Londonshire in 1960. Doreen's father was high up in Customs and Excise so it was quite a change for Grant to go from Bo'ness Rebel to son-in-law of a C&E Officer over a period of less than 10 years. Doreen's family home was in Worlds End Lane, Chelsfield in Surrey, how home counties can you get? Amusingly Grant told me just before he was married he brought into the country from one of his trips a new Dining Room Suite but labelled it 'garden furniture' to get it through Customs free and clear.

15

The Caledonia Show Tours

During the summer of 1960 Flora Stuart Grubb, a highland dancer from Newcastle, NSW, Australia, was touring Scotland and competing at Highland Games up and down the country. Flora had been doing very well in championships in Australia and her local community had raised enough money to cover Flora's travel costs to Scotland to compete here. Flora had a grandaunt who lived in Linlithgow Bridge where she spent part of her time but she spent some time in Aberdeen while taking some coaching lessons from J.L. Mackenzie. My Mum had lots of distant relatives in Australia and we had offered to help by taking Flora to some of the games where I was dancing. We saw quite a bit of Flora over the summer. At the Cowal Gathering, the last weekend of August, Flora created a major surprise by winning the Adult World Highland Dancing Championship, the first overseas dancer to do so. After the gathering Flora travelled back with us to Bridge of Allan. She was due to go home to Australia after the end of the Highland Games season in September.

We received a phone call from Flora later in the week to say she had been offered an opportunity to join a Scottish stage show which was due to leave at the beginning of October on a five-month tour of the United States and Canada. She told us the group was also looking for a Male dancer and she had suggested they contact me about it. A few days later Andrew Macpherson, who was the Director and leader of the group, phoned and gave me more information about the tour and the people involved. He needed an answer within a couple of days because if I turned down the offer, he would need to find an alternative Male dancer quickly.

I talked the opportunity over with my parents and Willie Cuthbertson, who had trained me and was still a very good, wise and interested friend. Willie's advice was to consider it seriously but be aware that it would change my life considerably and would probably lead to conflict with my then employers and career plans (an apprenticeship in a Glasgow Chartered Accountancy firm).

Although I was intent on following my aptitude with figures and a life in finance, I felt it was an opportunity unlikely to arrive again so decided to take the chance, subject to agreeing my role in the show and the financial aspects. To go on a 16,000-mile tour of the United States and Canada at someone else's expense and to be paid to do so was too much to ignore. I managed to arrange with my employers a period of absence but with the understanding that I would return to the firm after the tour ended.

The above is a copy of the Contract for the tour, (original dates October 4th, 1960 to February 2nd, 1961) at a Salary of $100 per week, an absolute fortune to me at that time, even allowing for me paying the cost of food and accommodation during the tour. Thereafter a mad month followed of rehearsals three times a week for the show, and measurements, plus many fittings, for a completely new kilt outfit, Dress Stewart kilt and hose with a Bright Red Jacket plus silver buckled black Waistbelt, Sgian Dhu and white, silver mounted Dress Sporran. It was very important that the jacket while close fitting gave me the ability and room to move my arms in the normal Highland Dance positions without riding up or becoming uncomfortable. As it happened the company which had been asked to tailor the group's outfits was the famous Glasgow firm of R W Forsyth, ladies and gent's outfitters, in Renfield Street (but no relation to me).

I found out later that Dixie Ingram, from TVs White Heather Club, was originally booked to go on this tour but pulled out as he was tied to the Andy Stewart Show (Dixie was married to Andy's wife's sister). Andy had a new Show about to start touring Moss Empires circuit throughout the UK after his very successful TV series The White Heather Club and Dixie was his lead dancer.

The group was due to fly out to New York on October 4th from the old Renfrew Airport but there were some technical problems with the aircraft and the airline decided to move the group to a hotel in West Kilbride for the night. The following morning, October 5th, we were advised that we had been transferred to a British Airways flight to New York leaving from Prestwick Airport later that day. At the airport we were handed boarding tickets and duly climbed aboard the flight. Imagine my surprise when I was shown into the first-class cabin. Whether by chance or by design I was flying first class to New York on the day of my twentieth birthday, what a birthday present.

Most of the motels and hotels we used offered double, twin and triple occupation rooms so for the following five months I shared a room with Sinclair Little, the Piper and Joe Burke, our

Accordionist. Sinclair was from near Aberfoyle and Joe was from Bowhill in Fife just a few hundred yards from my grannie's house.

This tour was the first time I had been away from home for longer than a week or two so was quite a new experience for me. By the age of 19 I had travelled a lot around the UK and Europe but I had not really been responsible for organising my own day-to-day life. Most of the Andrew Macpherson Chorale singers on the tour were seasoned performers in shows in Scotland, some even had husbands/wives and children back home, but like me had taken the opportunity of a lifetime to tour Canada and the United States for a few months at someone else's expense. Some went on to make a career in the business on a larger stage. Margaret Savage, one of our singers/dancers, starred as a principal singer in the TV 'Black & White Minstrel Shows' in the later 1960s, and became a well-loved singer in the U.K. One of the girls on the second tour ended up as a soloist with one of the German Opera Companies. Others were seen and heard regularly on TV and Radio programmes.

of The Singers and Dancers of Scotland proved irresistible wherever it was presented, and the audiences clamored for more. Wrote the Milwaukee Journal: "CALEDONIA! will be welcomed back in any season."

In part the success of CALEDONIA! can be attributed to the zest with which the company performs. In the words of the Providence Journal, "A more exuberant and happy group is seldom seen." In large measure, too, its appeal lies in its exquisite singing and the brilliance of its dancing.

Above all, however, is the sustained magic of its performance, which holds the audience rapt from beginning to end with its pace and variation of mood. So deep is the rapport that, to quote the Vancouver Sun: "With the whole audience joining in the singing of Loch Lomond and Auld Lang Syne, a production vivid to the eye and ingratiating to the ear reached a great climax."

So spectacular has the success of CALEDONIA! been on our shores that, even before its first tour was completed, the demand for its return resulted in a second tour planned for season 1961-62.

The enormous enthusiasm it has aroused here runs parallel to its career at home. Founded by its artistic director, Andrew Macpherson, The Singers and Dancers of Scotland enjoyed a meteoric rise to popularity in their native land. Today they are a household word and enjoy sold-out houses wherever they perform.

They made their television debut about two years ago, in a program viewed throughout Great Britain. As a result, their popularity spread beyond the border and they became established favorites in the new medium. Quickly their reputation spread across the seas, and a tour of the United States and Canada became inevitable.

What makes CALEDONIA! entirely different from similar presentations is its imaginative staging and programming, coupled with artistic perfection and an unquenchable elan. In creating this production, Mr. Macpherson sought out leading soloists throughout

It is interesting that for the second USA/Canada tour the cast was substantially different with Joe Burke and I plus two of the girls the only ones remaining from the previous year.

The tours covered virtually the whole of the East, North, Mid-West, Western, and Southern states in the USA plus Toronto, Calgary, Edmonton, Victoria and Vancouver in Canada.

While still in the first week of the shows, travelling around the New England States, I went out for a walk in the neighbourhood prior to one show, but wearing kilt and tweed jacket. I was approached by one of the local policemen who obviously thought I was a tourist. While talking he asked what the 'thing' was sticking out of my stocking. When I said it was a Sgian Dhu and showed him that it was actually a four-inch knife in a sheath he nearly had a fit and said he should arrest me for carrying a concealed weapon. Luckily, he accepted my explanation that it was part of my standard highland dress and, after hearing I was in town performing in the Caledonia Show, he agreed that, as long as I put it away when I got back to the hotel, he would forget all about it. Needless to say, the Sgian Dhu was packed away never to come out again in public in the USA.

The group travelled around in the typical USA Greyhound bus, which you see in all the movies, only this one was cleared of the rear seats which were replaced with hanging rails for our show outfits.

The Caledonia Show Tours

Apart from a few flights to cover the longer journeys to Calgary, Edmonton and Vancouver in Canada, and one in Oregon in the US North-West, the bus became our 'Iron Lung' for our five months on tour as we travelled up to 250 or 300 miles per day.

In the USA it was mainly a 'Concert Tour Series' audience, as we were following up on performances by the Mantovani Orchestra, James Last Orchestra, Jose Greco's Spanish Dancers etc. with the addition of a number of University and College Theatres. In Canada, however it was definitely the Scots-Canadians, with many, many highland dancers in the audiences. In Edmonton I was told after the show that the whole of the balcony area in the theatre had been taken up by highland dancers. Thank goodness I didn't know that prior to going on. Everyone has nerves before a show and that is not what you want to hear when you are out to entertain, not necessarily to show top-level technique. However, it was one of our best audiences and they really showed their appreciation of our efforts.

In Victoria on Vancouver Island Joe Burke, our accordionist, and I took the opportunity to visit Heather Jolley's dance school. Heather and her Mum, Mrs. Duncan, also a great dance teacher, were regular visitors to Scotland during the summer championship season.

On the first tour we performed at least six times a week and seemed to spend all day in the coach. A typical series of shows over fourteen days in October/November was:

23rd Milwaukee, Wisconsin
24th Faribault, Minnesota
25th Shenandoah, Iowa
26th Big Springs, Nebraska
27th North Platte, Nebraska
28th Sterling, Colorado
29th Travelling
30th Cortez, Colorado
31st Greely, Colorado
1st Travelling
2nd Logan, Utah
3rd Salt Lake City, Utah
4th Bountiful, Utah
5th Twin Falls, Idaho

According to Google the direct route from Milwaukee to Twin Falls would be around 1700 miles long, but the route we took was anything but direct. From Wisconsin we went north into Minnesota, south into Iowa, west into Nebraska, south-west into Colorado, west into Utah and finally north into Idaho. Just the journey from Sterling to Cortez in Colorado was over 500 miles, hence a 'travelling' day, not a 'day-off'. Try following that on a map and you will realise why, over the whole tour, it's estimated we covered in excess of 16,000 miles.

We travelled down the West Coast through Washington and Oregon, eventually to Sacramento in California then on to the 'City by the Bay' San Francisco. A number of shows were scheduled in the greater San Francisco area so we were based in a hotel on Geary Street, in the city centre. At that time the Highland Dance teacher in San Francisco was Stewart Smith, who also ran Scottish

Country Dance classes in the city. At the hotel I received a note from Stewart saying that he would be in Texas when I arrived but, if I had time to look around the area, his car was at my disposal. When I got to his home it wasn't just 'a car' but an open top Ford Mustang, the kind of car that every young man would drool over. I thoroughly enjoyed driving it around but was shocked to find the overnight parking rate in the city was almost as much as my room cost, nevertheless, absolutely worth it, I was living the dream.

On a night off a couple of us managed to visit the 'Top of the Mark', the Cabaret Room in the Mark Hopkins Hotel which has amazing views right over the city. My biggest regret was that I missed, by just a few weeks, performances there by Nat King Cole, one of my favourite singers.

It was also in San Francisco that I found out that I liked Pina Coladas. While in a restaurant/bar on the Pacific Ocean waterfront of the city I was persuaded to try it as I didn't drink whisky (or much else to be honest) and it is made from a clear, no scent, white rum spirit. From then onwards that was the only spirit I would touch.

Los Angeles and Hollywood was the next major stop and there I met up with some dancing friends from the area, Barbara Burner and family, John and Cathy Hynd, Nan Daley and the Roberts family. On the second tour after the show some of us ended up at a party in the Roberts house which didn't end until it was almost dawn. Sometimes a day in a coach is useful.

From California the Caledonia Tour Shows moved on to Arizona (plus a quick visit to the Grand Canyon and a Navajo Indian Reservation), New Mexico (more Cowboys, Santa Fe and Albuquerque) and down the Texas Panhandle to the Houston area. From Amarillo to Lubbock to Abilene to El Paso to San Antonio, Cowboys all the way with a spoken drawl that was very difficult to follow.

I discovered I had left my tweed kilt jacket in the motel in Albuquerque, which in itself was not a problem, but my passport was in the inside pocket. A phone call made the necessary arrangements to have it sent on to the designated hotel in Houston. Meantime we were in Laredo right on the border with Mexico. After the show we were invited to go with the local UK Consul to a party across the border in Nuevo Laredo. When the missing passport was brought up, the Consul just carried me across the border in his car which had Diplomatic plates and was waved right through. With a mixture of Scottish and Mexican songs and dances it was a truly magnificent night.

On the first tour, after Houston, we travelled along the Gulf Coast and made our way to Sarasota in Florida where we had a couple of weeks off over the Christmas and the New Year holidays to rest and recover.

On starting again, we covered Florida, west and east coasts, and then travelled to Atlanta in Georgia. There I had a real eye-opening experience. Bear in mind this was in the early 1960s. In the city I used a local bus service and for the very first time found that I was the problem. At that time even the seating in the buses was segregated and I sat upfront while anyone of colour had to go to the rear of the bus. It is an experience that I have quoted on many occasions when someone talks about inequality or bias in the past. This wasn't a history story, it was my experience, in my lifetime, in a major city of the USA.

The remainder of our tours took us back up the east coast states to eventually finish in New York again.

The Caledonia Show Tours

We zig-zagged all over the USA and found out just how big that country was, but there was the benefit of seeing the places we only dreamt about at home. The 'Old West' of the Cowboys is real and alive in Nebraska, Wyoming and Utah. Names like Fargo, one of the stops on the old Pony Express route, and the Forts at Laramie and Cheyenne all came alive for us.

Life in the major cities like New York, Washington DC, San Francisco and Los Angeles showed the diversity of the States and how life changed from East Coast to West Coast, and what the Americans called 'the flyover' states, the Mid-West, were different once again.

What were the highlights? Well, the views on our arrival over the Golden Gate bridge and into San Francisco has to be one of them, while walking down the 'Walk of Fame' on Hollywood Boulevard with the names of all the great showbusiness big names in stars on the 'sidewalk' was pretty special. Standing in the little piazza in front of Grauman's Chinese Theatre, where the Oscars Presentations used to be held, meant we were 'on the red carpet' or at least in our dreams.

Washington DC, the nation's capital was very much a 'political city', a bit lacking in vibrancy and atmosphere but you could spend weeks there viewing their amazing collection of Public Buildings, Museums and Monuments; The White House, the Congress and Senate Capitol Buildings, the Washington Monument and the Lincoln Memorial, not to be missed, and we had enough time to see many of them.

I suppose in many ways, this was my 'coming of age' experience. Away from home, responsible for myself in clothing, meals, nights out (when possible), but most of all travelling with a group of similar minded people trying our best to entertain huge audiences, most of whom still had the 'Brigadoon' vision of Scotland.

At the mandatory receptions afterwards, it was my first impression of Americans as a people and how they lived in their own world. I have to say I haven't changed my opinion that if it doesn't make money then the general business-class people in the States just don't want to know. Aspiration to improve yourself is a good thing but not at any cost. The tours were truly eye-openers.

16
My Favourite Music & Songs

I have always loved music of all kinds though, for obvious reasons, Scottish Dance Music has been a big percentage of my own collection of CDs, DVDs and Albums - you know, the discs that go round and round at 33rpm on a turntable. It seems that Vinyl is making a comeback so maybe the LPs in the loft are worth some money now.

When you look through my collection it covers everything from Pop Music to Classical and everything else in between. Way back in the 60s and 70s it was mostly pop and rock classics but as the years went by the range expanded to include Country Music, Soul and R&B, Easy Listening and Classical plus of course most of the 'Anthem' bands such as ABBA and the BeeGees.

When I was in my late teens the POP music culture was moving from the United States to the UK with bands such as Cliff Richards and the Shadows following the 'Elvis Presley' style route into the charts. The clean-cut image of 'Cliff' was in contrast to Mick Jagger and the Rolling Stones, I was never a fan of them. UK pop was moving from Crooners like Frankie Vaughan and Jimmy Young, to boys with guitars like Cliff, Tommy Steele and Billy J Kramer then, during the 60s, the Fab Four, 'The Beatles' took over the British music scene then did the same in the USA. While I loved most of the earlier Beatle's music, I lost interest when they went into their psychedelic period. Incidentally, I once shared a theatre dressing room with a band called Joe Brown and the Bruvvers, who were big in the 1960s.

By this time I was listening to Paul Anka, Neil Sedaka and Roy Orbison, the Beach Boys, Everly Brothers and the Supremes, in other words back to USA mainstream POP.

While in the States I heard a lot of Country Music on the radio although it was generally talked of as Country & Western then. It probably started with Hank Williams, then I added Johnny Cash, Loretta Lynn, Kenny Rogers, Glen Campbell, Jim Reeves and Patsy Cline, all internationally known. I loved folk like Crystal Gayle (Don't it make my brown eyes blue), Lynn Anderson (I never promised you a Rose Garden), and Emmy Lou Harris (Sweet Dreams),

In some circles the Canadian singer, Anne Murray, is included as a country singer, but she is so much more than that. I have quite a few of her albums. Probably best known as the singer of 'Snowbird', she crosses over many different types of music and song. In a similar vein I love the music of brother and sister duo 'The Carpenters', who lived too short a life.

For an outlier I enjoyed listening to Bach's 'Magnificat in D', after being part of a combined local area Churches choir performing the chorale section and parts of Handel's 'Messiah' when I was about 12 years old.

On the more Traditional music side my cupboard has many albums by the Battlefield Band, Blair Douglas, Freeland Barbour's Occasionals, and many Scottish Dance Bands, including the Jim MacLeod Band and the Iain McPhail Band.

For obvious reasons I have Tannahill Weavers and Piperactive CDs as Kenneth played with them and other Scottish folk bands.

Many of the more recent CDs which I have collected were purchased to source tunes and arrangements which might have been useful for dance items in the Royal Edinburgh Military Tattoo, though truth be told, most didn't inspire me enough to use many of them, only Dougie Maclean and Blair Douglas made it into the Tattoo.

With such a large collection in the house, I generally now use iTunes if I need to play a track, so do I still need that cupboard? Well, when checking the names of tunes and bands a printed cover still comes in useful.

My Favourite Music & Songs

17

Winning the World Highland Dancing Championship

Winner of the Adult World Highland Dance Championship and, on the same day, winner of the MacLean Trophy for best Adult Dancer of the year, the only occasion when the MacLean Trophy was decided by competition.

Cowal Gathering is the major annual event in the Highland Dance Calendar. It now runs over three days up to the last Saturday in August, but during my compctitive career covered just the Friday and Saturday.

For all the competing dancers whether from Home or Abroad it causes the butterflies to flutter and the nerves to start jangling. Whether you drive by car over the Rest and Be Thankful and down the side of Loch Fyne through Strachur and Glenbranter to Dunoon, or take the shorter journey from Central Scotland across the River Clyde from Gourock on one of the Passenger or Car Ferries, there is an excitement to the journey as the anticipation builds towards the ultimate competition in Highland Dancing and the most prestigious prize of them all, The World Championship title.

Winning the World Highland Dancing Championship

I have seen, over the years, a number of dancers who could and probably should, have won more of the precious Cowal Medals, but could not cope with the expectation and pressure of dancing on the most famous platforms of all before probably the most discerning audience of all, gathered together in the stadium grandstand.

Over the period from 1960 to 1963 my life had changed completely and I had become much more confident in my ability to perform at the top level and entertain audiences through regular summer Highland Games events and many stage and television performances in Scotland and Overseas.

It was, nevertheless, with some trepidation I once again approached the entrance to the Cowal Gathering Stadium, suitcase in hand, containing my now well recognised Red Jacket with Black Epaulets and Dress Stewart tartan kilt, the outfit first worn on the 1960 Concert Tour of Canada and the United States. I had had a very successful competitive summer season to that point but in Dunoon it would count for nothing. The performance on the day was what mattered and now it had to be at the very highest level. As I entered the Stadium and made my way to the male changing room under the main grandstand, I was told that my main rival in the Championship entry list (at least in my estimation) had strained an ankle the previous week and was not able to take part in the competition. It was a lightbulb moment for me. Up until that point I had doubts but from then on, I was certain that I would end the day holding the World Championship Trophy. I have read over the years of other sports people having a similar experience, without knowing why, just that they knew that they would succeed that day. In a TV interview many years after it happened Alan Wells, the Scottish sprinter who won the Olympic 100m Gold Medal in Moscow in 1980, said the same thing. He knew before the race started that he would win it.

It was a tough day. It had been decided that the Brigadier Alastair Maclean Trophy, which was donated to the SOBHD for presentation to the top dancer of the year, should that year be awarded by competition and this event was first on the agenda. It was followed in the afternoon by the World Championship event which at that time was decided over three dances, Highland Fling, Sword Dance and Sean Truibhas, as at the time the Reel was not deemed to be a Solo Dance.

As the Prizes and Trophies were being presented and it became obvious I had the main one, my mother came running over the track onto the grass to grab and hug me (much to my embarrassment at the time). It's polite to wait until after the presentations before celebrating a win.

It was a very eventful day. As a special extra bonus, we had for a long time a real appreciation of the Shotts and Dykehead Pipe Band and their Pipe Majors, J.K. MacAllister and his sons and for years followed the band as it joined the Parade from the Stadium down to the town Centre after the Games finished. With the World Championship Trophy and the Maclean Trophy I proudly marched in front of the Band with their guys carrying their Trophies through the crowds lining the main street to the Queens Hall entrance.

When we reached the canopy over the entrance the Band formed a circle and Pipe Major J.K. told me it was my turn to perform. So the first time I danced after winning 'the Worlds' was to the music of a full Pipe Band in the town centre of Dunoon.

The day wasn't over, however, for in all the excitement I had forgotten that my suitcase and my travelling clothes were still in the male dressing room under the grandstand at the stadium. Cue: reverse my triumphant march down the Dunoon main street, and get back to the stadium before they all shut up shop, locked the gates and went off home. I'm pleased to say I made it in time.

There is no doubt that my Championship win in 1963, followed by a repeat win in 1964 changed my appreciation of what Highland Dancing can do to boost your confidence and instill a feeling that anything is possible if you work at it. I had the benefit of dancing full-time on two tours of Canada and the United States followed by taking part in numerous stage and TV shows and series which meant my fitness level was at its peak and my concentration had been established at a high level to ensure every time I performed it was at a good standard. With two 'Worlds' under my belt I was sought out for many different shows and later when I went back to dancing on a semi-professional basis, I continued to receive requests to perform on a regular basis.

When I established 'Billy Forsyth Scottish Dancing Shoes' (as a result of being unable to find a commercial shoe I felt comfortable in) the strapline in our advertising 'Made by a World Champion for those who would like to be World Champion' was a great advantage.

At Scottish Television it took me from 'one of the dancers' to Dance Director of one-off shows such as St Andrews Night Ceilidhs, Burns Night events and Hogmanay Parties, and later a whole series of shows, working with many of the great TV stars of the day.

Dancing Through Life

THE VIEWER—December 21, 1963 Page 55

7.30 EMERGENCY—WARD 10

with
JILL BROWN
DESMOND CARRINGTON
PAULA BYRNE

CAST:
Carole Young .... Jill Browne
Chris Anderson ..... Desmond Carrington
Frances Whitney .... Paula Byrne
Andrew Shaw .... John Line
Lester Large .... John Carlisle
James Gordon .... Michael McKevitt
Dr. Fitzgerald .... John Arnatt
Sister Doughty .... Pamela Duncan
Michaela Davies .... Tricia Money
Kate Ford .... Jane Rossington
Matron .... Enid Lindsey
Tim Bush .... Fraser Hines
Dr. Beckett .... Geoffrey Colville
Sarah Smith .... Rona Rodgers
Elizabeth Brenkan .... Sheila Fearn
Jean Twilfoy .... Elizabeth Murray
Harold de la Roux .... John Barron
Sister Mills .... Beatrice Kane
Sister MacNab .... Dorothy Smith
Nick Williams .... David Butler
Jill Craig .... Anne Brooks
Phillips .... Robert Palmer
Night nurse .... Anne Ogden
The New Year is seen in at Matron's Ball—but in Ward 10 there's a crisis.
Script by Basil Dawson
Directed by Phil Brown
Produced by Cecil Petty
An ATV Production

1.0 THE ALFRED HITCHCOCK HOUR

starring
BARRY SULLIVAN
in
Day of Reckoning
with
Guest Stars:
CLAUDE AKINS   KATHARINE BARD
HUGH MARLOWE JEREMY SLATE
K. T. STEVENS   LOUIS HAYWARD
CAST:
Judge David Wilcox ...... Louis Hayward
Dr. Ryder .... Les Tremayne
The District Attorney Robert Cornthwaite
Dr. Camphill .... Alexander Lockwood
The Coroner .... James Flavin
The Court Clerk .... Tom Begley
Frazier .... Buck Taylor
The police officer .... Hinton Pope
Felicity Sampson .... Dee Hartford
An architect and his wife have a violent quarrel on board his yacht. He pushes her ... she falls overboard. Should he try to save her? And if he doesn't, who would ever know he was responsible?
A Scottish Television Presentation

.55 NEWS

University Challenge Answer
Harry Champion (they're all music hall songs)

9.10 FOLLOW THE FUN
Irresistible Miss Bullfinch
starring
BARRY COE   BRETT HALSEY
GARY LOCKWOOD
Guest Stars:
Amanda Bullfinch .... CELESTE HOLM
Charlie Finnegan .... ALAN HALE
When Amanda Bullfinch was young, her father broke up her romance with Charlie Finnegan, a maid's son. Now, 20 years later, her father has died. And Amanda sets out to trace Charlie—despite determined opposition from her relatives, who expect to inherit the Bullfinch fortune.
A Scottish Television Presentation

10.5 WORLD IN ACTION
At the end of a year of bitter confusion, the most distinguished commentator on North American affairs
ALASTAIR COOKE
takes stock
Narrated by Derek Cooper and Wilfrid Thomas
Executive producer: Tim Hewat
A Granada Production

10.35 NEWS HEADLINES

10.37 SCOTSPORT SPECIAL
1963 has been one of the most exciting years for football since the war. The last Scotsport programme of the year recalls some of these great moments—among them, the Celtic-Rangers Scottish Cup Final, Scotland's magnificent win at Wembley, and Dundee's bid for European Cup honours.
Edited by
Arthur Montford and Doreen Paterson
Directed by Ian Dalgleish
A Scottish Television Network Production

11.3 FRANCIE AND JOSIE
starring
RIKKI FULTON as Josie
in
The Odd Job
with
ETHEL SCOTT
CLEM ASHBY
GLEN MICHAEL
CHARLIE SIM
DOUGLAS MURCHIE
ALISTAIR AUDSLEY
BRIAN JONES
JACKIE FARREL
DAVID EAVIS
Unbelievable. But it's true. Josie goes job-hunting with Francie's Cockney cousin. They land up in a mystery house on a deserted Scottish island with the strange and sinister Dr. Yes, their employer. What has he in store for them?
Scripts by Stan Mars
Designed by Arthur McArthur
Produced by Liam Hood
A Scottish Television Network Production
(See Page 22)

Bomber Gascoigne hosts another session of "University Challenge" tonight

11.33 PERSONALITY OF THE YEAR
'The Viewer' Annual Award
The presentation of The Viewer award to the Scottish Television Personality of 1963
(See Pages 21 and 23)

11.45 HOGMANAY PARTY
JIMMY NAIRN
Introduces
MOIRA BRIODY
JEAN CAMPBELL
ROSA GOLDIE
DOROTHY PAUL
ALASDAIR GILLIES
BILL McCUE
PETER MALLAN
THE CUMBERLAND THREE
THE JOE GORDON FOLK FOUR
Piper:
WILLIAM BRYCE
of The Black Watch
and
THE CLYDEBANK LYRIC CHOIR
Conductor: Alra Graham
with
BILLY FORSYTH and the DANCERS
and
JIMMY BLAIR and his BAND
Musical director: George Kiernan
Continuity: Campbell Lennie
Designed by Hildi Rae
Produced by Liam Hood
Directed by James Sutherland
A Scottish Television Network Production
(See Page 22)

12.30 LATE CALL
Calling on you this week: the Rev. Dr. R. Selby Wright, Church of the Canongate, Edinburgh
A Scottish Television Production

Close down

Patients in Ward 10 can rest assured tonight—for Dr. Frances Whitney is on duty

Winning the World Highland Dancing Championship

18
'The Shoes' From Whence They Came

It's the real story - honest. Why would I tell fibs*?

Once upon a time - well all good stories start that way.

Many years ago, back in the early 1960s actually, I was seeking a new producer of highland dance shoes. I had been using the famous 'Finnegan' shoes since I was a very young competitor but the remaining shoes had finally worn out completely and the Finnegan family were no more, so where was I to go for a quality product. I had tried a number of different products but not been completely happy with any of them.

A friend had recently had a pair of shoes hand-made for him and to say the least they were not what I would have wished. To my surprise while walking round a Highland Games field with him one afternoon he introduced me to a young man with the words "this is the guy who thinks your shoes are terrible" Oops! A diplomat he was not. The craftsman, for that he certainly proved to be, didn't go bananas with me but asked what I felt was wrong with the dance shoes he had produced. A long discussion ensued and he offered to make me a pair to the specifications I was demanding.

So commenced a long period of trial and error to achieve a shoe which would give me the shape, flexibility, support and durability I was seeking without the drawbacks common in other shoes of the time. After constructing some six or seven pairs, each amended and adjusted to gain a higher level of quality, comfort and fit, I eventually agreed he had produced a shoe to meet that most demanding breed of dancers, the contenders for top championship titles, and there were many vying for the major honours, most now widely recognised teachers and judges.

It was inevitable, of course, that I was asked by other competitors on the Highland Games circuit where I had found the new highland dancing shoes - oh and could you get me a pair! Although we did not have the large numbers who attend the major championship events these days, there was a regular group of leading dancers competing at Gatherings up and down the country on a weekly basis and all were, and still are, friends, no matter how the week-to-week results turned out.

Have you ever tried to get cash out of friends? I left my wallet in the car/with mum! My husband has my purse and has gone off to watch the cycling/running/heavies! I've no change I've just bought wee Jimmy an ice cream! But I'll see you next week anyway, I'll let you have it then!

Yes, I know, but they were, and are, good friends, honest! So there were never any doubts about obtaining payment - eventually. And all this for twenty-nine shillings and eleven pence a pair, that's £1.50 in today's currency.

Problem solved. I took £10 of prize money from one of the Gatherings and started the "shoe float" to cover the cash flow problem - and the rest is history!

Now we export to every major country in the world. We send shoes to dancers in Banjul as well as Bathgate, Toronto as well as Troon, and we even sent a pair of large size 11s to Alaska - personally, I'm convinced they were worn over the snow shoes!

Wherever Scottish Dancers perform, from Karachi to Kobe, Toronto to Tokyo, or just Motherwell to Machrihanish, you'll see the distinctive cut and style of the Champions Choice, the dance slippers produced by a World Champion for those who would like to be Champions.

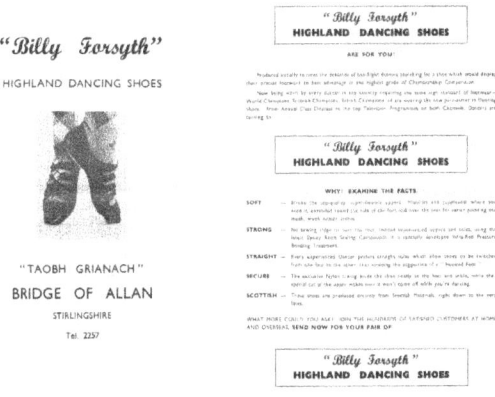

Thank you to all my friends in dancing for their support over the years.

*the Scottish equivalent of "economical with the truth" or "that's not my understanding of the meaning of that word"

In 2014 I decided that it was time to hand over the reins to 'the Shoes' and it happened that my son Colin and his wife Nicky had decided to move back to Scotland from New Zealand, good timing. Colin and Nicky took over the business and at last I was free to travel on extended trips knowing that 'the Shoes' would continue in their hands.

'The Shoes' From Whence They Came

19
Flying High with British Caledonian

Having danced as a Guest with the British Caledonian Airways Pipe Band a few times I was asked to join the team involved with their Airline Promotions overseas on their African, North, Central and South American routes.

For special occasions such as St Andrews Society Dinners and Rabbie Burns Night celebrations the Airline would send two or three Pipers and a couple of dancers to add to the evening's Entertainment.

For other events such as the first flight on a new route the Airline sometimes transported a whole Pipe Band and Dancers. As a result, I found myself quite a few times travelling to the Airline base at Gatwick from Glasgow on the first flight of a Sunday morning, returning on the early afternoon flight after dancer/piper/band rehearsals, in conjunction with dancers local to the London area. Neil Strath, Malcolm Lay, Pat Reid and others had performed at Pipe Band events around London but the overseas trips were mainly done by myself, Malcolm and Derek Chisholm (from the Duns area of Southern Scotland). I had another Australian connection at this time when Joy Alder, a highland dancer from Canberra, spent the summer in Scotland and I persuaded her to join our little concert party in the London area for a few months. Much later Gareth and Deryck Mitchelson also danced for B.Cal Airways on a few overseas trips.

For a period, I was on the first B.Cal flight from Glasgow to Gatwick on a Saturday morning, transferred there to an international flight around 10 or 11 am and within a few hours I was basking in sunshine in West Africa, the Southern United States, or on the west coast of South America. That was the wonder of time travel, especially going west with the sun, when you could depart Gatwick at 11 am but on arrival in Dallas/Fort Worth in Texas it was still only early afternoon. A quick recce of the venue and discussion with the hotel management then some quiet time before getting dressed for the evening entertainment.

Generally, those events finished about 11 pm but occasionally the festivities could go on till the early hours of the Sunday morning.

As always it was back on the evening overnight flight from where-ever to Gatwick and then onto the first flight to Glasgow arriving Monday morning about 9 am. I could leave the office on a Friday evening travel to Africa, South America or the USA over the weekend and be back in my office by morning tea time on the Monday.

It was quite normal during those years for my colleagues in the office to ask on a Monday "OK which country did you end up in last weekend?"

B.Cal ran flights to Banjul in the Gambia, Freetown in Sierra Leone, Atlanta, Dallas/Fort Worth and Los Angeles in the USA and to Puerto Rica in the Caribbean, Caracas in Venezuela and Quito/

Guayaquil in Ecuador. I visited quite a few of those destinations and others through B.Cal.

I own a pair of real down-to-earth tooled leather Cowboy Boots, bought from a real authentic Cowboy Boot Store in Mexico City, as a result of being there with B. Cal. I have never worn those boots again since I returned home. The boots have three-inch-high heels, which was the principal reason for buying them in the first place.

Derek Chishom and I were dancing at the major Mexican Saint Andrews Society Dinner in the City. As always, we performed a few dances over the evening, during and after dinner. I made the major mistake of showing-off at the end of a Sean Truibhas demonstration by finishing with a couple of big leaps. As I landed after the second one, I heard a snap and when I went to walk off the floor found that I couldn't really use my left leg. In panic I signaled frantically (but with big smiles) to Derek to come on to the floor and take over the demo while I gave him a big build up for his next dance. As soon as the focus was off me, I moved slowly to the side of the floor and out of sight. The hotel managed to get Ice and cold towels to me but my trip was over. Trouble was I could still hardly put any weight on my left leg. My normal Ghillie brogues were no good so with the help of our local expatriate Scots we hunted around for some footwear which would allow me to get around. The only thing that helped was a boot with a raised heel so a visit was made to a local boot shop. You guessed it, hence the pair of Mexican Cowboy Boots which now lie unused in my shoe cupboard. If nothing else a souvenir of Mexico City and a reminder to me not to show-off.

In Puerto Rico in order to promote the Inaugural Flight B.Cal had sponsored a horse race at the local track and sent the whole Pipe Band with a couple of dancers. On the Sunday we all ended up at the track although I don't think the racegoers really appreciated the sound of the Bagpipes or a performance by us Highland Dancers. They did appreciate the colourful tartan outfits though and the Press were well represented so the publicity people were very happy.

On a different visit, to Quito in Ecuador, more than 10,000 ft. high in the Andes Mountains, this time with Malcom Lay, our small group of Pipers and Dancers was invited to visit the Monument which marked the Equator some 15 miles outside the city. We were told there was a plan to build a new big Visitor Centre to replace the modest marker which stood there and it might spoil the current simple symbol at the Centre of the Earth. Now was a good time to go.

Dancing Through Life

On the way back to the city we stopped for an early lunch at a restaurant which looked like an old Abbey Church. It was surrounded by grounds and orchards with many different and varied kinds of fruit trees. Malcolm and I picked fruit off one unusual tree and bit into it to taste the flesh which was somewhat like a pear type of texture but more bitter. Neither of us fancied the taste.

It was the usual quick weekend trip but this time leave London Friday to overnight in Guayaquil, on the coast of Ecuador as at that time there was no night flying into the airport in Quito in the mountains. Fly up to Quito Saturday morning, set up in the afternoon with the hotel staff for the Scottish Dinner in the evening. Imagine trying to explain to the local native South American Indian hotel chef, with little to no English, how he is going to parade into the dining room 'The Haggis', held high by him on a silver platter, proceeded by two Pipers in full No.1 Uniform complete with feather bonnets, and escorted by two tartan kilted Highland Dancers bearing Broadswords and the Society Chieftain holding two bottles of very precious Scotch. It was, to say the least, confusing but we got there. The following morning was the visit to the Monument on the Equator then back to Quito and to the airport for the afternoon flight out which went overnight to London.

That was one of the most desperate flights Malcom and I had ever taken. The flight crew were brilliant, no problem there, but what can you do when you spend most of a long overnight flight vomiting in the toilets. It can't have been pleasant for the other passengers either as we occupied those toilets for far too long a period. It was so bad that on arrival back at Gatwick Airport, the Customs and Immigration people were seriously considering whether we had picked up some South American disease rather than food poisoning and put us in quarantine for most of the morning. We did eventually make it to our homes later that day but swearing never to try unwashed, unknown fruit ever again.

I claim to have danced the Highland Fling at a higher level than anyone else in the world (except Malcolm Lay, who was with me at the time). On a flight from Gatwick to Dallas, after the dinner service, the chief Stewardess announced over the intercom that there were special guests on the flight, Pipers and Dancers from the Airline's Pipe Band. A few passengers then started asking for a tune and a dance so after checking with the flight crew and making sure the other passengers didn't mine, Malcolm and I did a quick switch and put our kilts on, the pipers brought their pipe boxes down from the overhead lockers and tuned up and the two dancers put on their dancing shoes. At 33,000 ft up in the sky on an aircraft flown by Captain N Parker (never forgot his name) we danced the highest ever Highland Fling as we were travelling at more than 500 mph over the Atlantic Ocean.

Now I use that experience to bamboozles the kids with the problems of dancing on an in-flight aircraft travelling at hundreds of miles per hour. You see, you start off in the aisle at the front of the cabin and every time you hop (and there are a lot of hops in a Highland Fling) it takes you down the aisle a little bit as the aircraft moves forward, until at the end of the dance you are actually at the opposite end of the aisle. It's simple logic, isn't it? Oh! and is that the fastest Highland Fling as well?

One of the fringe benefits of being part of the regular B.Cal. promotions squad was an annual opportunity of staff-cost tickets for myself and the family to a B.Cal destination. Thus, we visited both Puerto Rico in the Caribbean and the Gambia in West Africa for holidays, and made some great friends with the local expatriate population (mostly Scots) which lasted over many years.

20
My JFK Moment

On Friday 22nd November 1963 I was due to dance at a concert in Harthill, Lanarkshire, which is on the old A8 main Glasgow-Edinburgh Road about midway between the two cities.

I had met Ronnie McLennan, leader of the Harthill Country Dancers, at one of Archie McCulloch's Indoor Highland Gatherings in the Kelvin Hall Arena earlier in the year where they and I were performing. Later he contacted me and asked if, as a favour, I would dance at his St Andrews Night Show in the village. (I had just won the Adult World Highland Dancing Championship).

When I arrived at the venue the place was buzzing. The news had just come through that John F. Kennedy, the President of the USA had been shot during a motorcade in the city of Dallas in Texas just an hour or so previously. Not much information was available and it was not known whether or not he was still alive. As you can imagine speculation was rife as to the ramifications for international relations, especially after the USA-Cuban crisis and the sailing towards Cuba of Russian warships.

I don't remember what was on the programme that night but as with many of my age I still remember exactly where I was when Kennedy was shot.

I was in the USA on tour with 'Caledonia' when Kennedy was elected in November 1960 and still there in February 1961 when he was inaugurated, and it seemed everyone loved this new, young, President with his 'chic' wife.

My JFK Moment

I suppose JFK's 'big' moment was in October 1982, taking the decision to face up Russia and dare Khrushchev, with his ships containing ballistic missiles, to break through the US naval blockade of Cuba. It seems the leaders of both countries recognised the possibility of a nuclear war and publicly agreed a deal to de-escalate the situation.

Henceforth any potentially life-changing major decision became a 'JFK Moment'.

What was my JFK Moment?

Well, I think, undoubtedly, it was my decision to sign the contract with Andrew Macpherson's Caledonia Show in September 1960 and commit myself to leaving my job with the accountants in Glasgow and go travelling around the USA and Canada for five months over the Autumn/Winter of 1960/61.

From that decision led another one to continue in the entertainment industry and go on the following Caledonia tour of the USA and Canada in 1962. There was no going back then and through the contacts made during that period I ended up dancing in stage shows up and down the country and in television series for Scottish Television and BBC Scotland TV and on the UK Networks.

When, a few years later, I did go back to semi-pro status, I continued to dance on stage and perform in dinner and cabaret shows while moving back into Finance roles at different companies.

I was Finance clerk at Forthvale Rubber Works in Stirling, where my dad had worked many years before. I moved to the Finance Department at the National Coal Board Offices at The Whins in Alloa. I then moved on to be Cost Control Officer for the Tractor line at the massive BMC truck plant in Bathgate, then on again to Donbros Knitwear in Alloa, originally to the Finance Dept but, on arrival, asked to review the raw materials handling and distribution systems. I remained there in control of raw materials for about seven years before finally moving to become Finance Officer at Scottish Youth Hostels Association headquarters in Stirling.

I'm sure none of this would have happened if I had not signed that contract with Andrew Macpherson.

Where would I have been? No-one knows but I would not have had nearly as much fun as I eventually have had, that's for sure.

My JFK Moment

21
Best photograph I've ever had taken?

The photograph shown here was taken, I believe, in 1966, by a local photographer Ian Kennedy, who at the time had a small studio near the top of Baker Street in Stirling at the 'Top of the Town'.

It was taken as part of a series to produce some publicity photos for use in promoting myself and my dance group, the Allan Water Dancers, for shows and events both on Stage and on Television.

Best photograph I've ever had taken?

The other group photo used extensively from that shoot was this one below. The original was shot in full colour but I no longer seem to have a copy of it.

The black & white version was used in postcard form with contact details etc. written on the back and our name across the bottom of the front.

The four girls in the picture danced with me for a few years, three of them lived in Harthill and the fourth in Fauldhouse, just over the hill from there. All were members of Ronnie McLennan's Harthill Country Dance Group whom I first met at an Indoor Highland Games show staged by Archie McCulloch, in the Kelvin Hall Arena in Glasgow. When I was Cost Control Officer for the Tractor line at BMC Bathgate we had a house in Macdonald Crescent, Armadale, the girls were local and quite happy to join me and have the opportunity to dance in a wider range of shows around the country. They certainly did that, from Aberdeen in the north to Leeds down in England, plus the odd TV show.

The location of the shoot was just off the Causewayhead Road from Bridge of Allan towards Stirling, in the grounds of what became the University of Stirling, to be precise behind the house which stands alone along that stretch of road.

Why was this my best photo? Technically it's ok but not brilliant.

For competitive purposes I would be incorrectly dressed. No Bonnet. But as a statement about Scotland, Scottish History and Scottish Culture it ticks all the boxes. Vibrant and colourful, a Scottish man dancing ancient steps against a background of a Scottish Hero, what more could you seek?

It was used almost as a stock photo for a number of years, including one year on the front of the main tourist guide for Stirling. For me it became the go-to photo for promoting appearances in shows.

Never underestimate the difficulty of producing a photo of a Highland Dancer in a pose which is generally acceptable to other dancers. The arms are wrong, the supporting foot is turned in, the leg is not straight, the kilt doesn't swing like that, you name it, they all have a reason to say it's not right.

The problem can sometimes be simply that the angle of the dancer gives the wrong view and hence positional problems.

Over the years I've had hundreds of photographs taken while dancing, some ok, but mostly terrible, and there's nothing you can do about it. The Press will print what they have and move on to the next story.

Ian Kennedy came up with the ideal photograph, at the right time, and I can't thank him enough for that.

Best photograph I've ever had taken?

22
RSOBHD Delegate, Chairman, President

Back in 1958 at one of the Highland Games I met an American lady from Long Beach, California, who was on holiday in Scotland with her daughter Barbara Sue, who was competing in some of the Highland Dancing events.

Barbara Sue was a very attractive teenager who I estimated to be about 16 years old. Not for the first time did I discover I had no idea about girls' ages. Barbara Sue was dancing in the under 14 years groups. With her long dark shoulder length hair, her 'well developed' figure and precocious approach to life, she could have been taken for a Scottish 17 or 18 years old anywhere.

As was a regular occurrence with overseas visitors they were invited to our house and we gave them the benefit of our knowledge of Games dates, dancing organisers and routes to the events. We helped Mrs. Burner to contact some of the dancing organisers to enter Barbara Sue in their dancing events.

I remember in particular her attempt to enter Barbara Sue for Tobermory Games on the Isle of Mull. We found a telephone number for the Secretary in the Scottish Games Association Annual Handbook and Mrs. Burner used our phone to contact him. We did not know that the Tobermory telephone exchange at that time was still a manual one. When the call went through it was picked up by the local operator there who promptly told Mrs. Burner 'you'll be trying to connect to the Games Secretary but he won't be at home at the moment, hold on and I'll find him for you'. A few minutes later Mrs. Burner was having her conversation with the Games Secretary and Barbara Sue was duly entered in the dancing competition. I suppose in a village of maybe around 500 or 600 inhabitants, on an island off the west coast of Scotland, in the 1950s, it would be reasonable for the local telephone exchange operator to know the whereabouts of the Secretary of the Highland Games a few days before the annual event but for Mrs. Burner it was the ultimate confirmation that Scotland really was Brigadoon in disguise.

As an aside, Mrs. Burner lived very close to the then relatively small headquarters of the Walt Disney Corporation, and knew many of the people who worked at Disney Studios and the new "Disneyland" complex (opened 1955). Many of her friends worked with the film studios based around Los Angeles.

On the first Wednesday of the Glasgow Fair fortnight Luss (Loch Lomond) Highland Games took place next to the small picturesque village on the shores of the Loch. At the end of the Gathering I discovered that Mrs. Burner did not have transport back to Balloch to the train station. I offered them a lift and put their cases on the luggage rack of my car as it was only a few miles. When we reached Balloch Station I discovered their cases were no longer on the luggage rack. Immediate mad panic as their cases contained all their clothing and their dancing outfits. We returned towards Luss driving much slower than when we came and to our relief found the cases on the grass verge. They had slid off the roof rack, without us even realising it, when we went round one of the corners. Panic over!

A few years later Mrs. Burner returned to Scotland with her younger daughter Judy to compete at the Highland Games and we became very good friends.

In September 1960 I had the opportunity to go on a five-month Concert Tour of the United States and Canada with the show 'Caledonia', incorporating the Andrew Macpherson Chorale (eight of whom also performed as dancers) with two lead dancers, a piper and an accordionist, a total group of 19 people. Our tour schedule took us from New York, up through the North-East states, across the Mid-West then into Canada to Calgary and Edmonton before crossing to Vancouver on the West Coast. We then travelled down the USA West Coast to San Francisco and Los Angeles, continued through Nevada, Arizona and New Mexico into Texas, then across the Gulf Coast and south to Sarasota in Florida, where we spent Christmas and New Year, before completing our tour up the East Coast back to New York.

We spent a few days in the L.A. area and were based in a hotel in Hollywood. When we arrived at the hotel there was a message from Mrs. Burner and the girls inviting us to a party organised by some of the local dance group principals at one of their homes. While Andrew Macpherson and a few others used their day off to make a quick trip to Las Vegas I was treated to a whirlwind tour of Hollywood and Long Beach including a visit to the original "Disneyland"

During the second Concert Tour, the following year, we were again invited by Mrs. Burner and the girls to join them on a free night to meet the local Scottish Society members for drinks and a meal. It turned into a very late night.

A couple of years later, in 1964, I was contacted by the secretary of the Southern California Highland Dancing Association, Nan Daley, and asked if I would be prepared to act as their representative at the RSOBHD meetings in Edinburgh. After I agreed to act as their liaison, a request to the RSOBHD led to my being accepted as the SCHDA representative in January 1965.

The Scottish Official Board of Highland Dancing was set up in 1950 to bring some order and consistency to Highland Dancing in terms of accepted technique, movements, steps and dances. Most of the innovations which had periodically appeared in Highland Dancing had been accepted by dancers all over Scotland, but from time to time in the early years of the 1900s, some exponents had introduced new variations of their own, which were only adopted by their own pupils. It meant competitive dancers had to change their style and steps when moving from one part of the country to another. The SOBHD was an opportunity to bring everyone together and adopt a common base.

I was in attendance for the first time at the March 1965 Meeting. It was extremely daunting when you consider those attending the meetings at that time included all the well-known Judges and Teachers of the day, Brig Alasdair MacLean, Dr Alistair MacLaren, Jack Muir, Jessie Stewart, Elspeth Strathern, Cissie Tucker, Willie Cuthbertson, Jean Ritchie, Miss Wallace, Christine Robertson, Ada Calder, both Jean and Mary Lindsay plus Sadie Simpson and various Competition organisers such as Baillie Councillor J.F. Stewart (Edinburgh Festival) and Hugh Mathieson and John Thomson (Cowal Gathering).

Overseas teachers and competitors were among those who attended the meeting of the Scottish Official Board of Highland Dancing held in the Carlton Hotel, Edinburgh. Included in this informal group are Mr J. Muir, chairman; Councillor John F. Stewart; Sheriff Bell; World Champion Bill Forsyth; Mrs Zelpha Wood, from Canada; and Joy Alder, Australian champion.

After the death of our President. Brig Alasdair MacLean in 1973, Dr Alasdair McLaren was elected President and I was asked to stand for the position of RSOBHD Chairman. I was surprised to say the least but was persuaded that I was one of the very few 'independent' representatives on RSOBHD and was not a member of any of the Examining Bodies thus giving me, in their eyes at least, an unbiased view of the various matters which came before the Board.

I was duly elected, and as I was re-elected to that position for many years afterwards, I assume that I carried out my duties to the standards they had set.

The Secretary of RSOBHD was Marjorie Rowan, (daughter of Cissie Tucker) and just a few years older than me. She was appointed Secretary/Treasurer of the RSOBHD (following Elspeth Strathern) and served the Board in that capacity and eventually as Director of Administration for over 50 years. She was a hard taskmaster who acted strictly to the rules and regulations of the Board. While her manner could be brusque, she always acted fairly and to the letter of the rules and the constitution. For many years she virtually ran single-handed the "World Governing Body of Highland Dancing" from the spare room of her flat in Forbes Road in the Bruntsfield area of Edinburgh. With a husband, three children, a full-time job and a dance school, she was a very busy person. Only after a move of her 'office' to a room rented from the Saltire Society in Atholl Crescent and the introduction of the Registration Schemes many years later, did she agree to take on a part time assistant.

In due course the Saltire Society moved from Atholl Crescent to a new location just off the Royal Mile and the RSOBHD needed to find a new office. After much searching, mainly by Marjorie, we found a former Locksmith's office at 32 Grange Loan, near Causewayside, one of the main roads leading out of the city on the south side, and with the help of a loan from the Bank became the proud owners of our new Headquarters, which we named "Heritage House".

Sometime before this I had approached David Ward, a graphic designer (who had worked with SYHA) with an idea for a logo for

RSOBHD. David produced the finished artwork, the now familiar Broadsword, Targe and World Map laid out as two overlapping discs, surmounted by RSOBHD lettering, which now appears on all RSOBHD material from Textbooks to letterheads and compliments slips.

Royal Scottish Official Board of Highland Dancing

In my earlier days as Chairman of the RSOBHD the Dancer Registration Scheme was introduced, originally for pre-Premier dancers but eventually to include Premier Dancers as well. The cards were printed locally on heavy card, with the dancers' achievements written onto them by the organisers of the competitions where they were successful. A pretty basic procedure. As experience was gained in the operation of the Registration Scheme it has been amended to suit the requirements of the Dancers' progression and the increasing numbers, and meet the practical needs of the Competition Organisers.

The system was extended to all our Overseas affiliated bodies making it much easier to integrate Premier and Pre-Premier Dancers from all areas of the world into competitions, no matter in which country they were held. In due course a plastic version was obtained then a new upgraded version of the RSOBHD Registration Card was introduced (in the style of a credit card) which allowed the production of them to be brought in-house.

Over these years the Board has also adjusted the points formula to establish the winners of Championships and Premierships, to better reflect the choices of the Judges. The system is based on three Judges for each dance who give each (and every) dancer a mark (out of 100). The Judges' score sheets are then taken to a team of Scrutineers, normally using a computer software programme, which identifies the top six dancers from each Judge and, using the points formula, produces the Dance Result. At this stage the formula is known as 'Dance Points'. When the four Championship or Premiership dance results have been compiled the top six placings from each dance are further scrutineered using the same points formula, at this stage known as 'Championship or Premiership Points' to produce the Overall Result of the Event. After much discussion over the relative value of the top six placings the formula now used is based generally on the 'golden number', with each placing worth roughly 1.666 times the next lower place. In theory this should give equal weighting to dancers given different placings by the three Judges, and more accurately show the overall opinion of the Judges Panel. A vastly improved system from the one generally used at competitions in the 1950s when it was four points for first, three for second, two for third and one for fourth.

One major reporting change which I instigated was the written and published Annual Report to RSOBHD Members. It had been the practice for the Chairman to give a verbal report to the Annual General Meeting which was then included as part of the Minute of the AGM. By providing a written and published Annual Report it was possible to include much more information on the year's activities.

For the first few years the Annual Report was a massive exercise printed off sheet by sheet in the print room of the SYHA at the back of the headquarters in Stirling. Cover pages were then printed and with a clear front sheet then began the task of assembling something in the region of 65 to 70 copies. A word of thanks here to the secretarial staff and print room manager at SYHA for a job, which they most certainly didn't have to do, but saw as their annual penance for having me in charge.

With the assistance of the various overseas affiliated bodies and their registration officers in the different countries it was also possible to include other statistical data including numbers of Dancers (in the different categories) and competition organisers registered, not just in the United Kingdom, but also around the world. For the first time RSOBHD had some real data on Highland Dancing participation around the world, albeit only on dancers registered for competitions. We also published in the Report the names and home city or country location of the winners of every Championship held world-wide during the year, an extremely valuable record for the future but, more importantly, at last an annual recognition by RSOBHD of our Championship winning dancers.

Before closing this essay, I must acknowledge again the amazing contribution to the RSOBHD of Marjorie Rowan, who in my early days 'In Office' made my life so much easier. As far as I was concerned Marjorie knew everything there was to know about RSOBHD, from the Rules and Constitution to the reason why X was possible but Y wasn't acceptable because …' here is what the Board decided when this or a similar situation came up in the past'.

While I tried to act in an Independent and non-controversial way and guide rather than direct discussions, I was very much aware of my esteemed predecessors who had Chaired RSOBHD meetings and the many distinguished Members who had built the basic systems from scratch to create a true World-Wide Governing Body. We have built on foundations laid by others and must not forget them.

In due course, as my working life with Scottish Youth Hostels progressed and I ended up as Deputy General Secretary and then Chief Executive of the organisation, I decided it was time to reduce my commitments. At this time I was appointed as an Independent Member of the RSOBHD.

During the following year our President, Dr Alastair McLaren, died and I was asked to stand for the position of RSOBHD President to which I was duly elected and held for some ten years.

In 2016 I was approached by representatives from the three teaching bodies (BATD, SDTA and UKAdance) and asked if I would allow my name to be proposed once again for the position of Honorary President. As it was put to me, there were a number of problems arising from alleged unacceptable activities and comments of the incumbent Honorary President and it was felt that she no longer had the confidence of those organisations. After consulting with a number of the other Board Members I agreed to this. In the event I was elected unopposed. On being made aware of my nomination, the then President withdrew her own nomination and immediately resigned from her position and all committees of RSOBHD.

As of 2023 I had been re-elected to that position at each following Annual General Meeting.

During my time in office, I was able to travel widely through Canada and the United States and to South Africa, Australia and New Zealand, adjudicating at Championships, Hosting Special Functions and Compering at many major International Highland Dancing events. It gave me a chance to talk to dancers, parents, teachers, organisers and adjudicators all round the world, and feed their views back into RSOBHD meetings in Edinburgh.

On one occasion, during discussions on some major changes to our Constitution and Rules and operating systems, I flew on a Wednesday from Scotland to Australia, arriving there Friday, held meetings with the Australian Board members on Friday evening, Saturday and Sunday, then left to return home on the Monday. It was a very short but very successful trip having allowed lots of time for questions about the changes and opportunities to show where the benefits of the changes would arise.

It is fitting that in its 70th year the Scottish Official Board of Highland Dancing was honoured by H.M. the Queen and given the title Royal Scottish Official Board of Highland Dancing.

RSOBHD Delegate, Chairman, President

23
Any serious accidents?

I have been relatively healthy throughout my life - after a few problems as an infant and youngster.

I can only remember one accident in which I received an injury although, that day, there was a more serious injury in the back of the car.

The story here is that I had finally managed to move up from an Austin A30 Van, first of all to an A35 next generation van, then to a brand-new Vauxhall Viva car. Vans were much cheaper than a car because, at that time, there was no purchase tax on a small commercial vehicle, as long as there were no windows on the sides behind the driving seat. The vans were economical for travelling, did a good job for me, and acted as overnight accommodation, if necessary, in an emergency, for my trips up and down the UK. The new car however, was my pride and joy.

It was a disaster therefore when, driving to Stirling one morning, only a month or so after purchasing it, I was faced with an unusual problem. The narrow back road from Bridge of Allan into Stirling, through Cornton and over the railway level-crossing, ran past the former Young Offenders Unit as you approached the Stirling Cornton houses. It then twisted back and forward for a half mile, skirting that housing estate, before straightening up and widening out into a standard two-lane road into the town.

As I drove round one of those bends, I was faced with a large flatbed truck, fully loaded with sacks of coal, coming straight towards me in the middle of the road, leaving no space to pass it.

Any serious accidents?

I had the option of driving off the road into the banking and a tall hedge, or come to a full stop in about five yards.

Neither happened. I swerved to avoid hitting it dead centre and managed to scrape past the cab but couldn't avoid the big double wheel at the rear. My upper front teeth came through my bottom lip where, inside, I still today have a slight cut, but otherwise I was only very shaken up with no major injuries. My passenger was not as lucky.

A few weeks before I had been presented with the Alastair Maclean Trophy as Dancer of the Year, and needed to have my name inscribed on it. I chose that day to put it in the back of the car to have that inscription done.

Unfortunately, the trophy was not restrained there and it was thrown forward with the impact of the crash to end up in three separate pieces on the floor of the car. I don't know whether I was more worried about the state of my car, or how I would face the RSOBHD Officials to explain how I had destroyed their new trophy.

Eventually of course, my motor insurance company replaced my car and the MacLean Trophy was pieced back together again. It took a while however, before I lived down that incident with my fellow dancers. As a result of the accident the RSOBHD agreed to have a foam-lined wooden case made to transport the MacLean Trophy so that it would never again be damaged should someone be careless enough to leave it lying on the back seat of a car.

My only other injury incidents have been when dancing.

Some years ago, I travelled to Copenhagen in Denmark as part of a Scottish Tourist Board presentation. We took over a whole floor in one of the main department stores in the centre of the city. A stage had been set up in the Restaurant area and during the Lunch and Afternoon Tea periods the group promoted Scotland and in addition to some Scottish Cookery demonstrations we performed some Highland Dances for the diners. Just a couple of days before the Promotion finished, while dancing a Sword Dance, I crossed over the blades but found that when my feet landed on the floor my body was still turning and I wrenched the calf muscle. While I managed to complete the dance, within minutes I was unable to walk and spent the next day, before travelling home, with my leg bound up and mostly resting on a chair.

The other dancing injury was a torn Achilles tendon during a display in Mexico City on a British Caledonian Airways promotional trip. It has been recounted elsewhere and accounts for the pair of Mexican Cowboy Boots sitting in my shoe cupboard.

For some years after those dancing injuries, I had the occasional tweak in my leg muscles and, of course, that is my excellent excuse for a perhaps 'less than great' technical performance in some shows, though naturally, it was covered by the smiling and always bright and confident public presentation.

Any serious accidents?

24
Scotdance Uncovered

As one of the most prominent names within Scottish Highland Dancing world-wide have you ever wondered why there is no mention of 'ScotDance' before the late 1980s? Let me resolve the mystery.

In the early 1980s I was asked to adjudicate at a number of Championships in Canada which led eventually to my being asked to host and compere the Canadian Championships for many years.

While in Winnipeg in the mid-1980s, after adjudicating the Mid Canada Championships, I was asked by the Organiser, Irene Baird, for a chat about the Canadian Inter-Provincial Championships, at that time run by a co-ordinating committee of which she was a member. Irene felt, due to the increasing importance of, and costs involved in, organising the series of events, that there should be a National Organisation in charge of it, and responsible for funding it. Before she could take the idea forward to the co-ordinating committee, she needed a basic form of Constitution and a name for the body. She knew that, as Chairman of RSOBHD, I had been involved in the changes and upgrading of the RSOBHD Constitution and Rules, and asked if I could offer advice on the way ahead.

In 1987 when we formalised the name of the organisers of the Commonwealth Championships held in Edinburgh's Princes Street Gardens (run annually from 1970 by Marjory Rowan and a few other volunteers including Cissie Tucker and Willie Cuthbertson) we set up 'SCOTDANCE' representing the 'Scottish Cultural Organisation for Traditional Dance, Music and Song'. If it was to receive Non-Profit status it had, under UK rules, to cover more than one form of leisure activity and thus Music and Song were added as they were used in the performance of Highland Dance.

In Winnipeg, by the next day, I had sketched out a constitution and come up with a name for it, 'The Scottish Cultural Organisation for Traditional Dance in Canada' or for short 'ScotDance Canada'. It seemed appropriate that a Canadian organisation should reflect the same ideas and ethos as in Edinburgh and would do the same job for dancers, teachers and administrators.

Maybe I was a bit naïve in thinking that would be the last I heard of the abbreviation 'ScotDance'.

The name was to come up more than once over the following years as the short-form 'ScotDance' was also used by New Zealand and later by the USA in promoting Highland Dance under the umbrella of the RSOBHD. Now, by the dancer numbers involved, frequently the word 'ScotDance' is quoted more often than RSOBHD despite it being relatively new on the scene.

To ensure some control over its use, many years ago I registered 'ScotDance International' in Scotland, as a company limited by guarantee.

25
Meeting Famous or Important People

I suppose the first question to ask is "How do you define Famous and Important". Is it by the position they held or the public profile they were given by the media or simply by how many people would recognise their name and say why they knew of them. On the basis of the last sentence here is my list, accepting that many will be unknown to the younger generation of readers.

In Scottish Showbusiness:

Billy Connelly (Film/Stage/TV/Radio Actor/Comedian/Musician) I only ever performed once at the same event as Billy. It was a special formal Dinner and Ball hosted by the St Andrews Society of Paris at a hotel in the centre of the city. Billy was their special guest for the evening and his stories and songs were widely applauded by the Scots in the audience, although, in truth, I am not sure that the French and Diplomatic guests of the Society actually understood any of his patter, spoken in his strong Glaswegian accent.

During the early 80s Billy was touring venues around Scotland. At this time the 'Man in Black', Reeve Whitson, was trying to persuade local authorities, the Scottish Tourist Board and many prominent individuals, that he could create a new 'Brigadoon' village somewhere in the Highlands if they would only give him loads of money to establish and support it. While in Scotland Reeve had been in touch with me regularly about dancing and producing shoes at his village, and he invited me to the Billy Connelly event in the City Hall, Perth. How he managed to do it I don't know but he had apparently spoken to Billy a few times about his project and had acquired tickets for the Perth show.

At that time, I was the Accountant at Scottish Youth Hostels and knew that Billy spoke in some of his performances about his experiences as a teenager in Youth Hostels. Not, I must add, in the most complementary terms. Typical Connelly, creating entertaining stories from everyday events and places. During the interval Reeve and I went backstage to speak to him, and my background, including my then current SYHA position, produced roars of laughter from him. Billy is famous for his long, convoluted stories about his life in general and his teenage activities in particular. Well as soon as he re-appeared on stage for the second half, he said he'd just been reminded about his visits on his bike to Youth Hostels around Loch Lomond and the Trossachs. He immediately started on a long monologue about his hosteling experiences. Of course, he knew where we were sitting in the audience and, after each dig at some perceived problem in the hostels, kept honing in on a very uncomfortable SYHA Accountant.

Rikki Fulton & Jack Milroy (Francie & Josie) Scottish TV/Stage/Film actor/comedians

They were featured regularly as a duo and on their own in many TV and Stage shows. For many years the BBCTV Hogmanay programmes would not have been the same without Rikki's 'The Rev I.A.M. Jolly' piece, a skit on the BBC's 'Late Call' five-minute religious programme, which aired just before the channel closed down for the night. Using the same set as that programme, with its big, black 'Mastermind' chair and formal backdrop, the doom-laden and so serious Rikki sipped away at his glass of water, not realising it had been 'infused' with Gin. As his words and actions began to reflect his growing sense of inhibition, he became more and more indiscrete.

Rikki was an absolute master of comedy. While I was told Rikki liked to work to a precise script, Jack was the 'off the cuff' half of 'Francie and Josie', the two Glasgow wide boys, who played it by ear in the spirit of the old Music Hall comedians. Typical Glasgow comedy long before Billy Connelly took it to the world. I never worked with them on stage but did some TV shows with them as lead presenters.

Kenneth McKellar, the leading Scots singer of the 1960s/70s

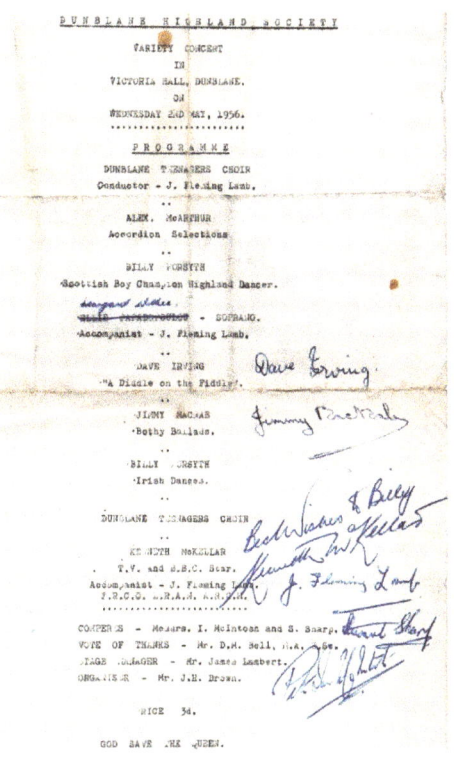

In spring of 1956 I was asked by Jimmy Anderson, the local Dunblane Jeweller who inscribed all my trophies, if I would dance at a Concert in the Victoria Hall, Dunblane. He was pushing the boat out and had managed to persuade the BBCTV and Radio star, singer Kenneth McKellar, to agree to sing at the show. Kenneth was still based in Glasgow at the time but did a lot of BBC Television shows and flew all over the world for performances. This was a major coup for a small town like Dunblane and the hall was packed for the special evening. The rest of the performers were locals including the Dunblane Teenagers Choir, Jimmy McNab, who sang Bothy Ballads and a young Alex McArthur on Accordion.

The Alexander Brothers, Stage and TV Duo, International Tours

Tom and Jack were just mid-twenties when I first met them. They had made a name for themselves in the winter Glasgow Metropole Theatre shows and, with youthful good looks and winning smiles, were favourites with 'more mature ladies', my Mum was a great

Meeting Famous or Important People

fan. I met them in various theatres and TV shows. Their big hit in the UK was 'Nobody's Child' but they performed many Scottish traditional songs including a load of the old 'Music Hall' ones such as 'My Big Kilmarnock Bunnet', Bonnie Wee Jeanie McColl, and Campbeltown Loch etc. Their version of 'The Dark Island' was always a great crowd pleaser.

Jim Macleod & his Scottish Dance Band

Jim was a local lad from Dunblane and his band comprised other local guys from around Stirling. Although only about twelve years older than me, I remember their broadcasts on the weekly BBC Children's' Hour Radio programme 'Down at the Mains', which provided a short, dramatic story about farming folk in the North East who then attended a Barn Dance where Jim's Band would play and various singers and folk groups would perform. Jim's band were also regular broadcasters on the BBC's Scottish Home Service dance music programmes and on many TV series with the

BBC and Grampian Television. Later he was also a regular annual visitor to Balmoral Castle to play for the Royal Family at their Ghilles Ball.

The original line-up was as above, Jim on Piano, Tommy Ford on Accordion, Chris Duncan on Bass, Jimmy McFarlane on Fiddle/Sax & Whistles and Alex McArthur on Drums, all from the local area.

Jim was based at Dunblane Hydro and was the Musical Director for Stakis Hotels all over Scotland. For many years, either on my own or with my Allan Water Dancers, I did a weekly half hour Cabaret performance during the Summer Tourist season at the Hydro. Over the Christmas and New Year holidays when the hotel was reserved for 'all-in' family packages, mainly from the Midlands and North of England, I would perform on Boxing Day and on New Year's Day, dancing Strathspeys and Reels to Xmas and New Year tunes such as 'Rudolph the Red Nosed Reindeer' and 'Jingle Bells'. When the kids were growing up and during their university years, despite those evenings being closed to locals, Jim always organised a reserved 'Forsyth' table at the back of the ballroom which the Forsyth family and friends, mostly student age, would fill with enthusiastic dancers. He knew that with so many non-Scots in the Ballroom he needed to encourage his visitors up onto the floor for his mixture of some modern, but mostly traditional

Meeting Famous or Important People

dances such as the Gay Gordons, Military Two-step, Canadian Barn Dance and Dashing White Sergeant. Who better than Billy's gang, who were also happy to partner some of the visitors and show them the ropes.

Sir Reo Stakis, the owner of Stakis Hotels, also owned a big, old mansion house next to the Hydro and would sometimes drop in to the hotel ballroom with his house guests who came from all around the world. His hotel chain included the Coylumbridge Hotel, near Aviemore, the Grosvenor Hotel in Glasgow and St Ermins in London. Thanks to Jim I danced in many Stakis Hotels at special themed evenings or on special occasions such as St Andrews Night or Burns Night. When Jim was invited to be the resident band on the cruise ship Canberra in 1986, he asked me to join him onboard as featured Dancer and Scottish Dancing Instructor.

Dancing Through Life

One amusing incident. Going off on holiday with the family one Friday evening I had to confirm something to Jim before departing. We drove up to the Hydro where I entered the ballroom just after the band had completed a dance. I could see Jim watching me as the dancers left the floor and I walked round the side of the room to reach him at the piano. His microphone was still on as I arrived there and his voice boomed out around the room 'Oh, it's you, Billy. I didn't recognise you; I've never seen you before with your trousers on'. It took a moment before the whole audience roared with laughter while Jim tried self-consciously to explain what was meant by his remark.

Strange that in all the years we had known each other he had never seen me other than with a kilt on.

Robert Wilson, the leading Scots singer of the 1950s

This was my first major occasion dancing for a general audience. My mother had read about a Charity Concert being held in the St Andrews Halls in Glasgow in April 1954 and had offered my services. At the time I was the Scottish Boys Champion which was (and still is) held at the Edinburgh Festival. To my surprise the offer was accepted and off we went to Glasgow. I had a rehearsal with Tammas Fisher, Robert Wilson's personal pianist, which I remember clearly as, while in the second step of the Sword Dance, he kept saying to me "Ok, Ok, can we do the quick time now" but knowing no better I continued until the proper entry into the Quickstep. He was a real pro and said how well I had done. During the show Robert Wilson himself gave me a big build-up

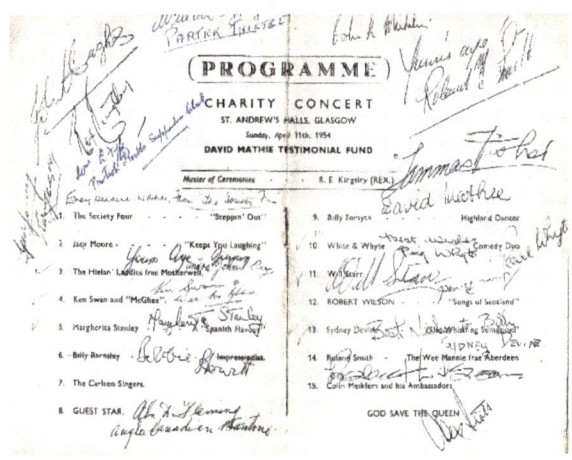

Meeting Famous or Important People

when I went on-stage and led the cheers when I completed my dance.

Jimmy Logan (Stage/TV/Radio Actor/Comedian)

Most of my TV work was through Scottish Television but I was asked to do a number of shows for BBC TV at their studios in Queen Margaret Drive, Glasgow, and on occasion on location at various venues. A couple of the TV shows were for St Andrews Night and Burns Night transmissions while others were part of regular series. One of them, when I danced a number with Aileen Robertson, included Jimmy Logan as host compere. Jimmy was not known for keeping to a script or the timetable and inevitably he started to ad-lib and the show ran over quite a bit. Jimmy was one of the stalwarts of Scottish showbusiness, having not just appeared on radio and television but in the summertime 'Five Past Eight' series of shows at the Alhambra theatre, which was generally followed by the annual pantomime starring him and Stanley Baxter.

Larry Marshall (& Kay Rose), STV Host and Comedian

Larry and Kay were TV regulars from the early days of Scottish Television. I performed with them in Jamie's Cabaret, a Dinner Show held in the then new King James Hotel at the top of Leith Walk in Edinburgh, where Larry was host and compere. I did two full summer seasons in Jamie's in 1973 and 1974 dancing solo spots and with Kay in the odd duet.

As a result of this and my earlier programmes with Kay at STV I ended up joining them for trips to London for a Boat Show Scotland promotion and to Canada.

During the Canadian trip we did a TV spot and found ourselves sharing the spotlight with a couple

146

of Oscar winners who had just returned from that big event in Los Angeles. Somewhere I have a photo of myself holding two Oscar statuettes.

Archie McCulloch (& Kathy Kay) Scottish Stage and Arena Show Producer

Archie was your typical show business impresario and the man behind the staging of Jamie's Cabaret in the King James Hotel, Edinburgh, amongst many other events throughout the U.K. He asked me to dance at various events around Scotland including a major 'Indoor Highland Games' in the Kelvin Hall, Glasgow during the Commonwealth Arts Festival of 1965 and another sponsored by a cigarette company. Archie's wife, Kathy Kay, was a regular singer with the Billy Cotton Band Show, a weekly BBC radio programme in the 1950s.

Other Scots included

Jimmy Neil and Aly Wilson, Variety Comedians

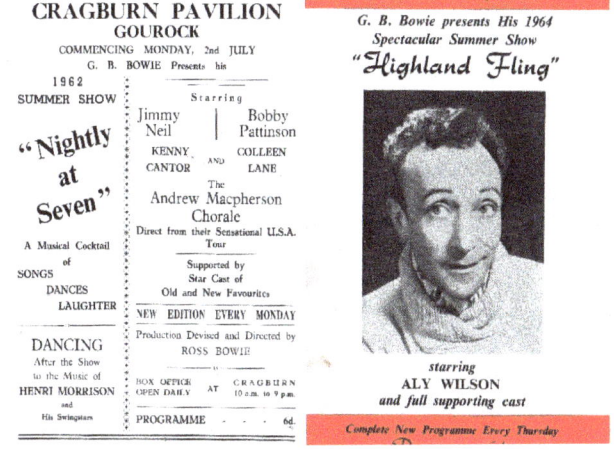

Bill McCue and Ian Wallace, Scottish Classical & Opera Singers
Dorothy Paul, Scottish Actress & Comedienne
Peter Morrison and Helen McArthur, Norman Maclean and Alisdair Macdonald

Meeting Famous or Important People

UK Personalities include:

Dave Prowse (former Weight Lifting Champion) centre figure in this photo

Dave really made a name for himself by landing the role of Darth Vader in the Star Wars series of films. He was also the caped Crusader on TV encouraging kids to learn and abide by the 'Green Cross Code'. Dave was a member of the group presenting the McVitties Highland Games in Tokyo and San Francisco.

Terry Hall & Lenny the Lion, 1960s TV Star, International Ventriloquist

It seems that each year STV felt the need to invite at least one major UK TV personality onto their live networked Hogmanay TV show (to attract UK non-Scottish viewers).

One such was Terry Hall at the time a leading international ventriloquist. During the rehearsals for the programme, the Director, Jimmy Sutherland, left his Control Box to pass on some notes to the gathered cast. During his chat he noted a couple of things for Terry but it was Lenny the Lion who actually answered him. To everyone's amusement Jimmy continued to have a long conversation with Lenny about his performance while everyone else was trying hard to control their laughter. When he eventually realised his position Jimmy laughed with everyone else. Lenny's well quoted catch-phrase was 'Aw don't embawass me'

Carrol Levis, 1950s & 1960s TV personality who hosted many TV Talent Discovery Shows long before Simon Cowell was even thought of

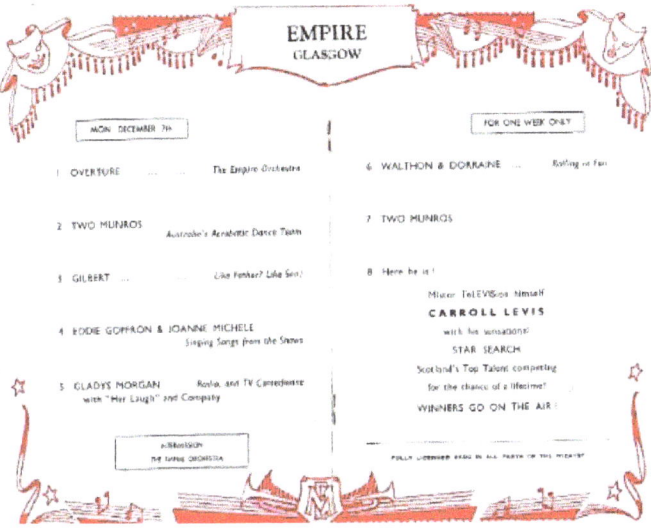

In 1959 with Janice Ingles, a highland dancer from Menstrie, who at that time was attending the Margaret Morris Ballet school in Glasgow, I auditioned for a spot in his Moss Empire show in Glasgow. We were selected from the early week show to dance in the final on the Saturday night but I think it was more to give some variety to the last show and avoid it all being singers.

Angela Rippon: BBCTV News and Programme Presenter (and a former dancer)

Through the Royal Edinburgh Military Tattoo, I was contacted and asked if I would take the Highland Ceilidh Dance Group to perform at a Charity Show in the London Palladium Theatre.

The organiser of the show was Angela Rippon one of the most famous of the BBC News and programme presenters. She kept an

Meeting Famous or Important People

eye on all the items at the show rehearsals and as a former dancer herself made a point of checking out our contribution.

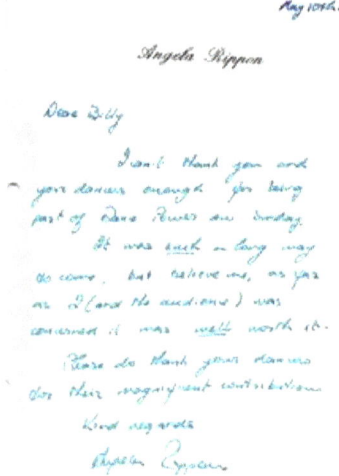

Hercules the Bear (with Andy & Maggie Robbin)

Does a Bear count as a personality? Well, he certainly got loads of press coverage over his lifetime. Bought by Andy as a very small cub from the Highland Wildlife Park, where they had no place to keep him and would have had to put him down, he was brought up as one of the family at the Sheriffmuir Inn, just a few miles up in the hills from my home.

Andy and Maggie bought the property and built a new outhouse especially for Hercules, but in truth he spent as much time in the pub as he did in his cage. I knew Andy as one of the wrestlers at the Highland Games and with my kids, we often went up to the Inn to say hello to Hercules. We watched him grow from a small cub to an eventual 70 stone, 9 ft tall Grizzly Bear, who was known all round the world for his wrestling antics with Andy, his TV adverts and his appearances in major movies on the Cinema screens as well.

Walter R Ballantyne O.B.E., Chairman and President Scottish Youth Hostels

Walter and his wife, Lottie, joined the SYHA in the 1930s and remained an active supporter of the organisation for the rest of his life. I met him many times after I joined the SYHA as Finance Manager in 1975. In my early days there, on many occasions I was sent with papers for signature to his home on the south side of Edinburgh. He attended all the Annual General Meetings, held traditionally at the Loch Lomond Youth Hostel, as long as he was able, and stayed there overnight with the rest of the members.

You may not at first be aware of Walter Ballantyne, but you would recognise his signature as he was for many years (1955-1965) the General Manager of the Royal Bank of Scotland and as such it was his signature on the banknotes issued by the Royal Bank.

UK Royal Family at various events.

H.M. Queen Elizabeth (Stirling Castle, Holyrood Palace, REMT)

Meeting Famous or Important People

Princess Anne, Princess Royal (REMT Rehearsals, Receptions)

Princess Margaret (City of Hamilton, Ontario, Official Reception)

Duke of Edinburgh (DofE Dinner Edinburgh Castle, Holyrood Garden Party, SYHA)

Prince Charles (now Charles III), (MBE Investiture, Buckingham Palace)

Prince and Princess of Gloucester, McVitties Games, Tokyo

Princess Alexandria and Angus Ogilvie, McVitties Games, San Francisco

International Personalities:

Telly Savallas, American Film & TV Actor (Kojac Crime Series & Major Films) He was a regular visitor to and house guest of Sir Reo Stakis, especially during major Golf Championships in Scotland. He was also of Greek descent although born and brought up in USA. One night, just before going on to do my spot for Jim Macleod at Dunblane Hydro, I was told that Sir Reo was in the ballroom with a guest from the USA. It turned out to be Mr. Kojac himself, Telly Savallas, although without his trade mark Lollypop from that TV series. He entered into the fun of the evening and even accepted an invitation to join me on the floor where we danced a Highland Schottische together.

Alan Jay Lerner, American Lyricist & Librettist (Brigadoon/ My Fair Lady/Gigi etc.)

When the 'Man in Black', as the kids nicknamed him, American Reeve Whitson, was trying to persuade the Scottish Tourist Board, Highlands and Islands Enterprise and various local authorities to back him with lots of money to create his vision of a Highland Village complete with hotels, restaurants and traditional goods manufacturers, he would turn up on occasion at our house in Inverallan Drive. He seemed to have access to just about anybody in Scotland who could influence the authorities, he was very definitely a good talker.

In 1983 he arrived at the house one day with an American guy in the back seat of his car and invited me out to meet him. The chap's wife, Liz Robertson, is a Scot, he said (although she was actually born in Ilford, Essex but that was near enough for Reeve.) I then shook hands with a rather ill looking Mr. Alan J. Lerner, the celebrated Lyricist who was the writer behind some of the world's most famous musical theatre shows. I discovered later that he had cancer and died just three years later in 1986. With composer Frederick Loewe and others, he was involved in Brigadoon, Paint Your Wagon, An American in Paris, Gigi, My Fair Lady, Camelot, Coco and On a Clear Day You Can See Forever, both the stage shows and the film versions. How Reeve managed to get him to Scotland and supporting a new 'Brigadoon' I'll never know.

As a final item in this story –

Representing SYHA I was invited to a Reception for Youth Organisations at Bute House in Edinburgh, home of the First Minister of Scotland.

While in the reception room with a glass in my hand, my mobile rang. As quick as I could I turned it on and whispered quickly "sorry can't speak now, I'm in Bute House with the First Minister and Sean Connery"

How's that for a put-down, it was true though.

26
Using the Mortgage Money

Back in the day Anne and I decided that we should build an extension to the house in Inverallan Drive to accommodate Anne's Mum and Dad, who were getting on in years and had some health problems. Anne was adamant that she couldn't share a kitchen with her Mum so we had a plan drafted to add a sitting room, kitchen, toilet and shower to the house linked to the fourth bedroom. To make it viable an Office and storage area was included for the Dancing Shoes business.

The plan was agreed with her parents and then passed the necessary local authority planning and building control committees. An application was made for funding and a mortgage was arranged. For some reason, probably the modest costs involved, the funds were organised and paid into my bank account just as the foundations of the new part of the house were put in place.

At this time I had been contacted by an American, called Reeve Whitson, known in our house as 'the Man in Black' due to his preference for very dark clothing, who was meeting people in authority up and down the country, promoting his idea of a specially built township as a showplace of Scottish culture and products. Reeve, from California, claimed his father had been a friend of Charlie Chaplin, had been involved in his friend's business activities, and as a result had a lot of money behind him. It seemed to me that Reeve had too much money, had watched 'Brigadoon' too often, and was somewhat obsessed with Scotland,

Using the Mortgage Money

however I was willing to listen to a possible location for making and distributing my brand of Scottish Dancing Shoes.

Reeve seemed to have the ear of everybody who had influence in Scotland and many in the Scottish Societies in California. On hearing of my involvement in the Vale of Atholl Pipe Band he suggested that the band should aim to play in California. Next minute we had an invitation from the organisers to visit the famous Santa Rosa Highland Gathering just to the north of San Francisco. As we laughed and said there is no way we can raise the funds to take the band over there Reeve said it could be done with sponsorship and he would organise it. True to his word he spoke with firms around the country and eventually was made an offer by Scottish Brewers, an arm of Scottish and Newcastle Breweries. Based on that he told me we should go ahead and organise flight details for the band. I had a travel agent who dealt with all my overseas trips so went to them and organised the flights.

The rest of the story has never been revealed before, and maybe should not be now.

As the trip came closer the travel agency required not just the names etc. of those members of the band going but also a payment towards the total cost to confirm the flights. As the trip came closer the funding from Scottish Brewers did not also come forward as arranged. Slight delay in the Accounts department was the 'reason'. On the deadline for payment the funds had still not come through from the firm and now my own reputation with the travel agents was on the line and I was constantly talking to Reeve who did not seem at all concerned. I had to make a decision.

The arrangements with the Highland Games had been made, the locations where the Pipe Band had agreed to play, apart from on the days of the Games, had been organised, and the band's accommodation at a US Forces base on Treasure Island in San Francisco Bay finalised.

I felt I had no option but to go ahead with the trip.

You're way ahead of me. To bring the two stories together,

Yes, I used the money in the bank designated to pay for the house extension as the payment for the flights from Scotland to San Francisco.

Yes, the money did come through from Scottish Brewers to put the funds back in the bank account.

Yes, the house extension did get built and Anne's Mum and Dad moved north into their new self-contained home, linked through into our house.

Yes, the trip was a great success, and the Vale of Atholl Pipe Band, later that year, were raised to Grade 1 status, an incredible achievement for a band whose personnel was very young, had a young Pipe Major guiding them, and had only been competing for a few years.

At the Gathering in the Sonoma State Fair grounds, the Pipe Band played in the competition, played a set on the main racetrack in front of the Grandstands for the general public, was featured on TV and gave a recital at a major evening function prior to the Games. The Band members ran riot travelling all over San Francisco from the base on Treasure Island.

During the visit the band members were also entertained to lunch at a ranch just outside the city where Gordon Duncan was asked to play for the horses and did so in his usual way.

Using the Mortgage Money

That trip was also the inspiration behind the 'skeleton lying on its back playing the chanter' logo when, in Boston Airport, Gordon decided to see if he could travel through the luggage screening machine and nearly gave the operator a heart attack when she saw what appeared to be a dead body coming through on her screen.

27

Taking After Mum or Dad?

Well, I've definitely inherited my Mum's obstinacy in terms of doing what I say I will do, even if and when it becomes difficult to do so, like her, I'm not one to give up if things don't run smoothly. I usually get there eventually although sometimes it requires a very persistent approach. Whether by choice or necessity I also have her ability to look at the statistics and make sure, especially on financial matters, that the figures do add up and make sense. I learned early on that if I wanted to buy something then it was up to me to raise the funds to do it, or alternatively make sure that I knew from where and when the finance was coming.

From my Dad I have inherited his quiet demeanor even if it does not always appear like that. One of the advantages of performing on stage is that effectively someone else takes over, someone who exudes confidence and can guide an audience to a desired outcome. To do that, however, requires a complete knowledge of your brief so a lot of preparation is necessary to ensure that happens.

I have to admit that I can lose the plot occasionally but it happens very rarely and only through extreme provocation. I always felt that my dad was like that too.

It's said often that Anne was the disciplinarian in the family when the kids were young, and that is probably true as she knew that I would only accept so much before raising the roof, and generally stepped in long before that would have happened. However, we were very proud of the fact that we could take them anywhere and knew that they would behave impeccably in company or at the many social and other events we attended.

Like Mum I am an organiser but where she tended to lead from the front, I have always tried to use the talents around me, I may have opinions but I realise that sometimes others have much better ones.

I am not a DIY person at all. I prefer to use what brain I have to work out the benefits of a project and use the best person for the job, and for household tasks that's just not me. So, I have not inherited my dad's ability to fiddle with machines and get them back into working order.

I think the most important trait I gained from both my Mum and Dad was the wish to improve my life and work hard to make that happen. Nothing is gained without effort but it does help if circumstances give you the opportunity to improve your position. It also means however, that you have to make the most of those opportunities, so again, weigh up the benefits and be aware of the dangers, but having made the decision ensure it gets your full attention, no half measures.

28
Joining the Military

In late **1991** the Secretary of RSOBHD received a call asking for a meeting of The Edinburgh Military Tattoo Production team with the RSOBHD Office Bearers. Marjorie and I attended on behalf of the Board. It was explained to us that it had been some years since there had been a display of Highland Dancing in the Tattoo programme and at this time the Scottish Regiments could not provide a large enough group of dancers for an item on the Esplanade. Could the RSOBHD possibly provide a team which could perform in an item alongside a large group of Scottish Country Dancers?

It would have been a dereliction of our duty to promote Highland Dancing if we had not accepted this challenge, particularly with our history of support from senior Military personnel, so Marjorie contacted the local Edinburgh dance teachers and arranged a meeting to explain what was required.

The Scottish Regiments had always been involved in Highland Dancing; it had been part of basic training in the Regiments from their earliest days. All Officers were expected to be able to dance and they had a certain style which reflected their upbringing. If not at boarding schools, because their parents were constantly being relocated to different parts of the world by the Army, then they gained instruction by their parents' own efforts when spending time on holiday at the Regiment's latest base. Within the Regiments the Pipe Major was the main dance instructor and many of them had been proficient dancers throughout their military careers. In my younger years I commonly met former military

Pipe Majors as Judges at dancing competitions in the Highlands and Islands. The first Producer of the Royal Edinburgh Military Tattoo was Lieutenant Colonel George Malcolm of Poltalloch, who judged many of my juvenile competitions at Highland Games, as did Brigadier Alasdair Maclean, Director and Producer of the Tattoo from **1951** until he retired in **1968**.

Many of the immediate post-war solo Pipers had served their time in the military and, as at that time many Highland Gatherings expected their prize-winning Pipers to play for the dancing competitions, we were treated, by some of the real piping greats, to the very best of music to show off our abilities. I danced to Wee Donald Macleod, John and Iain McFadyen, Donald Maclean of Lewis, the Mooch, otherwise known as Willie MacDonald, John D. Burgess and many more at the Gatherings in the North and on the West Coast. They knew what a dancer needed in terms of tempo and variation in tunes to give of their best, as they themselves had been dancers.

In due course a team of 16 dancers was recruited for the **1992** event. As the music for the item had been set for the Scottish Country Dance groups, the Highland Dancers were limited in the way in which they could arrange their part of the performance. In addition, because all Highland Dancing is off the ground the Tattoo team had arranged for mini platforms to be set on the Esplanade to ensure the Highland dancers avoided serious injury. The re-introduction of Scottish dancing into the programme was successful but it was not ideal as it gave little scope for us to show how Highland Dancers could use their skills to perform a wider range of movement and expression.

The arrangements for the two styles of dance to be included, one mainly social and the other mainly solo, continued for a few years during which Marjory gradually stepped back from being involved.

In **1996**, I was asked if I could provide a larger group of Highland Dancers for the following year, performing in their own spot on the programme and with a new more modern look and a more modern approach to the performance.

Thus the 'Royal Edinburgh Tattoo Highland Ceilidh Dancers' team was formed. The objective was to change how a large group of Highland Dancers performed, using the technical abilities of the dancers, to create a new and exciting 'Story in Dance'. To music specially written for us by the Director of the Scottish Lowland Military Band, David Thomson, and with a completely new look in dress, the 'Highland Ceilidh Dance' performed by 64 dancers plus a featured soloist, was a phenomenal success at the **1997** Tattoo. That music and dance became the Signature Style of the team and was used in many different programmes around the world. It showed how a large group of Highland Dancers could be organised to provide an exhilarating, colourful and dazzling routine which wowed the audience at every performance.

Over the following years the 'Highland Ceilidh Dancers' team performed in Scotland, England, Ireland, Canada, Australia and all-round Europe, including in a fantastic show in the Ajax Arena in Amsterdam before 60,000 people.

The highlights –

1998 the Scottish/Irish Dance year. The Producer had asked for a joint Irish/Scottish item showing the best of both styles of dance. He had invited an Irish Dance School from Dublin to perform at the Tattoo and we worked together to integrate the dancers from both countries.

1999 the 'Solo Drummer and Dancer' Dance, the choreography set a solo dancer and solo drummer together as a featured section of the dance

The Berwick Tattoo, REMT Dancers with the Scottish Division Lowland Military Band,

Ajax Arena, Amsterdam, Queen Beatrix's Birthday Concert, REMT Group with Ceilidh Band Ensemble from the Scottish Division Lowland Military Band and Pipe Major Ian Duncan. Headline artiste was Andreas Bocelli

Tony Cargill, one of our featured soloists

2000 the Dougie Maclean 'Perthshire Amber' Dance, the dance was choreographed and performed to selected sections and themes from Dougie Maclean's recording 'Perthshire Amber'.

The Royal Edinburgh Military Tattoo in Wellington, New Zealand, celebrating the New Zealand Arts Festival and the New Millennium. More than 160 NZ dancers were brought together by Mrs. Shirley Anne Thomson, who actually danced in the performance alongside her daughter and granddaughter. The New Zealand Academy of Dance had refused to assist in bringing dancers together for this event as they objected to working with myself. Although in NZ as Choreographer and Dance Director of the Edinburgh Tattoo, I was also the President of SOBHD, the World Governing Body of Highland Dancing, and the Academy did not recognise the authority of SOBHD.

It was to Shirley Anne's credit that despite that opposition & many other problems, she managed to bring together, from all over NZ, all the dancers required prior to the Tattoo rehearsals (Including where necessary accommodation with other dancers for the duration of the event.) I was presented with more than

160 dancers from age 9 to one or two who were, let's say, more mature Ladies, and we had three days to put together our spot in the programme.

I had arranged to start the item with teams of the youngest dancers (forty of them) performing their standard NZ Broadswords while the rest of the dancers, all 128 of them, came in from the four corners of the stadium. This helped me considerably as the dancers' own teachers made sure they were in place and on time. Splitting the group into four sections meant the routine was easier to teach and with some senior dancers helping younger ones, great progress was made. When we ran into problems because of a misunderstanding of the wording in the routine sent out in advance, it was simple to bring one section of the group together, review and amend the routine, then advise the other three sections. Despite time constraints the item was ready in time for the first performance.

The only big problem was the thunderstorm during the final Saturday night performance. Film footage showed the lights strung across the stadium swinging wildly in the wind and rain.

2001 Royal Nova Scotia Tattoo, Halifax Canada. The team danced their signature 'Ceilidh Dance' to the music specially written for this dance, and played on this occasion by 'Piping Hot' a pipes and ceilidh band combination from within The Invercargill (NZ) Pipes and Drums who were also in the show.

2002 the Queen's Golden Jubilee Royal Edinburgh Military Tattoo, the first Commonwealth Dancers year, with representative groups of Highland Dancers from Australia, Canada, New Zealand and South Africa.

United Kingdom Alliance Centenary Ball, Blackpool,

Performances with the Pipes and Drums of The Highlanders (4th Battalion Royal Regiment of Scotland) in the Top Square and in the Great Hall of Edinburgh Castle for a Reception hosted by the Duke of Edinburgh.

2003 The Sword Dance of the Great Wheels performed by the Highland Ceilidh Dancers and guests, the Schiehallion Dancers from Ontario, Canada, led by their Director Mrs. Sandra Bald Jones. The dance became one of the regular display items by the Highland Ceilidh Dancers, as it could be broken down into sets of eight or more dancers. It showed the intricate movement of all the Great Wheels of Scotland from the Watermill and Granary Wheels right through to the Wheels in the Railway Engines and Ships which Scotland supplied to the rest of the world.

RSPBA Northern Ireland, St Andrews Night Concert, Belfast

2004 the 'Wings' Dance year, celebrating the lead Service at the Tattoo, the Royal Air Force (and the Royal Australian Air Force). The REMT Highland Ceilidh Dancers are joined by guests The Ozscot Dancers from Australia led by their Director Mrs. Cheryl Roach

2005 the 'Sailing' Dance year. celebrating the lead Services at the Tattoo, the Royal Navy and Royal Marines. The Highland Ceilidh Dancers are joined by guest team the New Zealand Dancers from all over New Zealand led by their Director Mrs. Shirley Anne Thomson. The dance started in the outline shape of a Sailing boat and the patterns and formations reflected life and duties at sea.

'A Salute to Australia' in Sydney, NSW, a group from the Highland Ceilidh Dancers were joined by a group of over 100 Highland Dancers from Australia (organised for the event by Mrs Cheryl Roach)

The 'Netherlands National Taptoe' the Highland Ceilidh Dancers appeared alongside many international groups including the 'Imps' a young motor-cycle group from London.

This was also the year I remarried. Early in the year it was obvious this was going to be a busy one, there were only a few weekends without a function of some kind planned. Denise and I decided that if we were going to be married this year it needed to be done quickly. May was relatively free and we decided on the 21st but where?

On hearing about our decision, the Tattoo Producer indicated he could arrange that we have the ceremony at the Queen Margaret Chapel in the grounds of Edinburgh Castle and suggested that we ask the Tattoo Chaplain, the minister of the Canongate Church, if he would do the honours. We arranged to meet him only to find that was the start of the annual Church of Scotland Assembly in Edinburgh which he was required to attend. 'Don't worry', he said, 'I can attend the morning session of the Assembly, marry you during the lunch break, and be back down the road for the afternoon session, but I won't be able to come to lunch, sorry'. How cool is that.

2006 the 'Battle' Dance year. The Highland Ceilidh Dancers were joined by guest team the South Africa Dancers from all around South Africa led by their Director Mrs. Brenda Brett. The RSA dancers were brought in to the tune 'Nelson Mandela's Welcome to the City of Glasgow' moving down the Esplanade in the Bull Horn formation used by African Warriors when they went into battle.

Basel Tattoo, Switzerland, Highland Ceilidh Dancers appeared again alongside many international groups

2007 the Queen's Diamond Jubilee Dance year. Another 'Commonwealth' dance group incorporating 120 dancers from Australia, Canada, New Zealand and South Africa and of course The Tattoo's Highland Ceilidh Dancers. The dance was based on the Diamond Jubilee and included many and varied diamond patterns and finished with dancers in the form the 'Heart of Midlothian' a famous mosaic built into the cobbles outside St Giles' Cathedral on the Royal Mile.

60th Anniversary India's Independence – A Celebration Function in Glasgow

Netherlands National Taptoe, Rotterdam, a second visit to this major Tattoo

Fulda (Germany) International Tattoo, a team from Highland Ceilidh Dancers plus Ceilidh Band

2008 the Canadian Emigrants Dance year. Guest dance group the Canadiana Celtic Highland Dancers led by Directors Stephanie Grant and Stephanie Turnbull.

The dance showed the emigration of Scots to the new world and their life in that new environment. It concluded with the dancers from Canada and Scotland joining together as they do in the modern world, mixing and working with one another to everyone's benefit.

The Aventicum Musical Parade, this show is performed in the ancient open-air Roman Amphitheatre in Avenches, near Lake

Neuchatel in Switzerland. Apart from the incredible venue for the show, which had a simple dirt surface and as expected tier upon tier of space for the audience, the only thing of note was that one of the dancers fell during rehearsals and ended up with a plaster cast on her leg. Didn't stop her from joining in the festivities after the final show and trying to dance a Sword Dance over crossed crutches in a local bar. On the same flights to and from Geneva, and in the show, were members of the Boghall & Bathgate Pipe Band, not the competing Grade 1 band but a mixture of available players, who were determined to enjoy themselves on the local wine.

52 Brigade Reception, Edinburgh Castle

United Kingdom Alliance – Annual Conference (Blackpool)

2009 the Tam o' Shanter Dance year. If I remember correctly, on first seeing the outline of the dance the Producer said it was not quite what he expected. We had started by showing the gravestones of the extended Burns family and gone on to characterise

'*Warlocks and Witches in a dance,*

Nae cotillions brent new frae France.'

The very essence of Tam O'Shanter was the appearance of 'Auld Nick' and the ghostly figures in Kirk-Alloway, and it helped that the Producer had provided a 'Tam O'Shanter' riding on a real Maggie, his horse with a long tail, which hovered around the bottom of the Esplanade, watching what was going on.

With a detachable tail, pulled free each night by a tartan coated 'Nannie' it was great fun to perform. What the non-English speaking visitors and folks unaware of 'Tam O'Shanter' the poem, made of it all, I can't imagine.

The Windsor Royal Horse Show and Tattoo (Windsor Castle)

Fulda (Germany) International Tattoo, team from Highland Ceilidh Dancers with Ceilidh Band

This was a complicated year which started off with a health scare. After complaining of shortness of breath after returning from a walk down the farm track with the dogs I was sent by Denise to an appointment with Dr Mary Abercromby at the local Medical Centre. She was also a part-time heart consultant at Stirling Royal Infirmary and I found myself very quickly walking a treadmill there. After a few more tests I was diagnosed with a blocked artery and sent eventually to the new Edinburgh Royal Infirmary where they attempted to insert a stent. In the meantime, a long-planned visit to New Zealand (to visit Colin and Family) with my sister Andrea and husband Bill, had to be cancelled. The first attempt at the stent was unsuccessful however I was scheduled for a second try when the Surgeon had located and obtained the necessary extra 'wires'. This took place in mid-May, which leads directly to another story.

On the operating table only local anesthetics were required to insert the 'wires' into both groins, travel up the veins and clear the blockage, so I was fully awake while the work was going on. The position of the monitors and other equipment meant I couldn't see what was happening on the screens (other patients have said they could watch it all) so I was left to my own devices while the staff got on with it all. As the dance item for that year's Edinburgh Tattoo had not yet been organised, I found myself working out, slowly but surely, the entry, shapes, patterns, formations and dance steps routine for our spot in the show.

It surely must be the only time that a performance item for the Royal Edinburgh Military Tattoo was devised and arranged by a performance group leader who was undergoing a live operation in an operating theatre at Edinburgh Royal Infirmary.

2010 Celebrating the Royal Edinburgh Military Tattoo's 60 years by trying to show the changes in the Tattoo dance items over the years was a problem but resolved by bringing in at the start two of the current Regimental dancers demonstrating a basic Highland Fling. The dance then moved into a Strathspey and Reel, followed by adding in a section of the more modern style of presentation.

Voorthuizen (Netherlands) Military Tattoo

2011 the Fishy Dance year. As this was a year with Nature as its main theme, I was asked to produce a dance symbolising the Fishing Industry. I had a swarm of dancing fish, supported by the technical guys arranging an Esplanade that looked like part of the ocean.

2012 the Whisky Dance year. This was the year of Scottish Food and Drink. I was asked to promote the Scotch Whisky industry in dance with an item which covered the cutting of the barley, the mashing in the tun, and the distilling of the 'Water of Life'. We had a real-life Whisky Still in the middle of the Esplanade

At Garmisch Partenkirchen Tattoo, Germany, a full team from the Highland Ceilidh Dancers was invited to perform alongside German, French, and Omani Military groups.

2013 the 'Final Salute'. My final year as Dance Director of the Royal Edinburgh Military Tattoo. The Tattoo paid me the complement of, on the last night, bringing onto the Esplanade, at the end of our main spot, many of my past team members in a short reprise of the 'Highland Ceilidh Dance'.

Joining the Military

The girls added to the occasion by persuading me to join them in the Finale on the last night.

Although I was sad to retire as Dance Director, it was definitely time to do so. The previous year I had become rather short with some of the civilian back-up staff of the Tattoo, particularly the security ones. I understood the need for rigorous security but thought that after some 24 years with the Tattoo I had earned the right to some flexibility in my movements to and around the Esplanade during the four weeks of rehearsals and performances. It was concerning that the ever-changing security personnel were taking a 'jobsworth' view of their positions.

The Military is, and in many ways must be, a very inflexible organisation, and works to a strict discipline in all things, that's the way it gets things done, but the civilian staff tend to take on their roles as if they were a part of that organisation and assume powers that they don't have.

I showed over a long period that I had done a good job with the Tattoo and if I had gone on longer then I was likely to blot my copybook. I didn't want to do that and took the decision it was time to retire, still on good terms with everyone.

I was involved in the selection of my successor and was delighted that Aileen Robertson, whom I had known and worked with in the Highland Dance world over many years, was appointed to the post. Aileen has the background and knowledge, from a technical and presentation point of view, to do a great job there. How she will cope with 'the Military' and the male dominated hierarchy will be interesting to see.

Although officially retired from the Tattoo, I also took the opportunity of an invitation from the Brigadier in Charge of the Omani troops at the **2013** Tattoo, to have one more large group performance.

With the agreement of my successor, I arranged for most of the Highland Ceilidh Dancers team of the previous year to become my 'Scotdance International Team' of 50 dancers to perform at the Oman Military Music Festival, celebrating the Sultan's 50 years reign, in the Opera House Square, Muscat, Sultanate of Oman

With my Disney connections I also managed to organise an informal trip to Disneyland Paris for the final 2013 team members. It was a combined dancing, performing and holiday visit as a thank-you for all the hard work they had put in, some for a number of years, for me, and for the benefit of Highland Dancers everywhere. Over the years the group had shown that Highland Dancing can be more than just a competitive sport and could entertain, in small and large group performances, international audiences.

It is believed that 'The Royal Edinburgh Military Tattoo' is seen on television around the world by more than 100 million people each year. If so, that means our dancers have performed to more than 24 billion individuals around the world over my time with the Tattoo, and that does not include the many other shows performed during that time.

My thanks for those memorable opportunities go to:

- the Tattoo Producers, Major Sir Michael Parker (1992-94), Maj Brian Leishman (Interim 1994), Brig Mel Jamieson (1994-2006), Major General Euan Louden (2007-10), Brig David Allfrey (2011-20),
- to the many Tattoo Musical Directors (usually a new one each year) but particularly to Col. David Price (Scots Guards),
- and to the Pipes and Drums Directors: Major Gavin Stoddart, Major Steven Small, their successors,
- and to those in charge of the Pipe Bands and Military Bands, the Pipe Majors and Directors of Music, who enabled us to do our job, not forgetting the Military Ceilidh Bands who played for us for quite a number of years.

29

What invention has had the biggest impact on your day-to-day life?

One of the great mysteries of life is how young people, with no prior knowledge of an item, can immediately pick it up and seemingly with no fear and no inhibitions, start to use that item as if they had had years of instruction and education in how it works.

From babies in their cots with their toys, to teenagers with the latest must-have gadgets, they all seem to have an inbuilt knowledge of how to operate those things. Is this a modern ability or is it just a human being's natural inquisitiveness and a willingness to try anything. Whatever it is, the younger generations today have it off pat.

It's difficult to look back 40, 50 or more years and try to picture how I approached new inventions or equipment, without being over optimistic about my knowledge or ability at that time.

One thing I can do though, is recount the story of introducing a typing pool to the wonders of modern technology.

When I joined the staff of SYHA in 1975 we still had manual typewriters, although an electric model arrived there at about the same time as I did. SYHA had a system whereby an appropriate member of staff would act as minute secretary to each committee of the organisation. Those minutes would be written out or recorded on a 'dictaphone', typed up by an audio-typist (with a carbon copy

What invention has had the biggest impact on your day-to-day life?

retained in case of a problem), edited, if necessary, by the writer, passed to a typist to be retyped (with a carbon copy), then posted out to the Committee Convenor. In the majority of cases the Convenor would edit them again to meet their particular wishes on wording, then posted it back to Stirling. Here again they would go to a typist and be retyped onto a stencil for copies to be run off on the lithograph printing machine, located in an outbuilding at the back of the offices as it was noisy and ink tended to fly everywhere. No there were no quill pens around but there was a feeling that we were a bit behind the times in mechanisation.

Over the next few years, we added a few more electric typewriters, then I introduced an 'Amstrad' word processor as a trial, mainly to cut down the continual re-types. It proved a success so another 'Amstrad' was purchased. They cut down on the amount of paper copies being produced (and wasted) and was the first use of a storage disk although it was of very limited capacity.

Having moved to an electronic process the next stage was to introduce an IBM personal computer complete with built-in word processor and basic calculating program software. At that time IBM were way ahead of other digital processing firms although Apple did come out with a small personal computer which had a much more friendly interface. Eventually of course other manufacturers started producing 'PCs' and the 'IBM' part faded away. What a difference that made to the recording and production of meeting minutes. From there we added dedicated printers including ink-jet models, another new innovation.

As time passed it became necessary to look at a means of computerising the statistics of our Youth Hostels and the financial records. Once again it would be a major change to collate and disseminate the data produced at almost one hundred properties around the country where we had around 5,000 beds. Not only did we record total usage by month at every unit but also the breakdown by age category and country of our visitors, and of course the Income and Expenditure over a number of headings. After gathering information and specifications for probably a dozen different systems we finally purchased a multi-disk computer system for which we had to close off part of one office as a 'clean room'. Although at the time we did not have a dedicated person solely responsible for 'the computer room' it became evident that one would be required if we were to develop the system further. This we did, and by the time I retired from SYHA in 2001 not only were the internal operations of the organisation completely computerised and online but thanks to a very hard-working and dedicated young Computer Software Manager we had produced in-house specialist software and setup an online bed booking system, the first of any Youth Hostel Organisation anywhere in the world. A year or so before my retirement we demonstrated the system at an International Conference in New York by dialing into the SYHA headquarters computer from our laptop computer in the New York hotel and allowing one of our international colleagues to make a booking through the system.

Over a period of twenty-five years the SYHA went from manual typewriters to an online booking system available to anyone around the world with access to a computer. And all done (except for the hardware) by our own staff. Who says Scottish flair and ingenuity has disappeared.

Without doubt the advent of easily obtainable and relatively low-cost computers has been the most important factor in my business and private life closely followed, in recent years, by the use of mobile phones, which are more and more becoming mini-computers on which most activities can be carried out.

As a final word, I still believe that in the near future Highland Dance Championship Organisers, and in due course Ordinary Competition Organisers, will be handing out mini-computers to the Judges in order to more quickly and more accurately produce the individual and overall results from the Organiser's base Host Computer. No need to transfer dancer competition numbers or marks awarded to each competitor onto separate sheets to check and calculate Dance Points and then Championship Points. Input direct from the Judges leading to the final result.

What invention has had the biggest impact on your day-to-day life?

I have a feeling that the hold-up might be the user training necessary for the Judges and not the advancement in software engineering.

To go one step further, there is no reason why the Registration database held by RSOBHD should not be involved. When a dancer is entered using their Registration number, the Organiser's Host computer can download their details from the database and assemble the files to be used by the Judges, who will then have only their job to do, entering their mark for the performance, no more writing.

But not in my lifetime I imagine.

30

My Royal Connections

How many people can claim they have performed upwards of 40 times for Kings and Queens and their families? Well let me introduce you to one.

One of the introductions used for performers at Concerts back in the day was 'and has performed in front of Royalty and the Crowned Heads of Europe'. What that was supposed to mean nobody knows but it was the big build-up at many a function.

I must be one of a very few people to have actually been there and done that, performed in front of all the UK Royal Family and the Crowned Heads of Europe, not just once but many, many times, over many years. How can I be so sure? Well from the age of seven until I was in my mid-thirties, I competed annually at the Royal Braemar Gathering which was attended every year by the Royal family who at that time of year were resident on holiday at Balmoral Castle just twenty minutes from Braemar. This was a tradition which had been started in Queen Victoria's time and was continued by every Monarch after that.

Because of that tradition I had the opportunity to dance for King George VI and his family including the Dowager Queen Mary (wife of George V) plus Princesses Elizabeth and Margaret and their husbands the Duke of Edinburgh and Lord Snowdon. A few years later it was Queen Elizabeth and the Duke of Edinburgh with the Queen Mother and of course Prince Charles, Princess Anne, Princes Andrew and Edward plus later their wives and their families. On many occasions the Royal party included guests staying at Balmoral including some of their overseas family members and often UK Prime Ministers as well.

In 1955 at the age of 14, having won the Shield for the most successful Juvenile dancer I was asked to perform a Sean Truibhas for the Queen and the Royal Family. One Dancer, one Piper, facing to the Royal Pavilion (not the Judges), as the rest of the Arena went quiet for a few moments. No pressure there then as I went on the board to do my stuff.

Somewhere in the Press archives there is a photograph of a young Princess Anne waving to the boy dancers sitting at the side of the dancing platform, which was always placed directly in front of the Royal Pavilion. I was one of those boys waving to her and boy did we get told off by the Dancing Stewards for doing it.

Those days at Braemar were not the only occasions, of course. For a number of years in the late 50s and early 60s, during 'Royal Week' in July, when the Queen stayed at Holyrood Palace and carried out engagements around Central Scotland, there was held in the courtyard of the Palace, a Community Programme of Music and Songs to which a limited number of the public could obtain tickets.

An invitation came to the SOBHD to provide a team of Highland Dancers for those events. The team comprised four girls and four men including myself and the then Secretary of the SOBHD, Marjory Rowan.

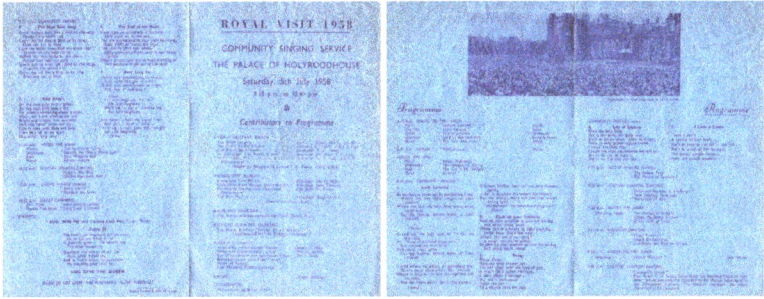

In later years I met the Royal Family on many occasions, representing SYHA (Scottish Youth Hostels, at the time I was Chief Executive) at the annual Garden Party at Holyrood Palace and at the Castle in Stirling during Royal visits there, and of course, during the Royal Edinburgh Military Tattoo where, over the years, many members of the Royal Family came to the performance.

Princess Anne was particularly interested in the Tattoo and attended a number of Tattoo events, including one of the rehearsals at Redford Barracks. When talking to her about the dancers and the dance I had choreographed for that particular year, the Queen's Diamond Jubilee, I made the cardinal error of saying the dance is of course based on Diamonds as 'Diamonds are a girl's best friend'. OOPS! She was not amused and gave me one of her 'Paddington' stares which you feel cuts right through you.

She was very interested in the dance items and always asked about the number of boys dancing in general and why there were rarely any in my Tattoo group. Truth is it was difficult to get boys of a suitable age who could commit to the rehearsal timetable and performances of the Tattoo which runs basically right through the month of August. The best I have managed to do is choreograph an item with a solo spot and bring in a pool of Championship winning soloists, including a few boys, who were each able to cover a few performances over the run of three and a half weeks.

In addition to the Royal Edinburgh Military Tattoo our Tattoo Dance Team also performed at the Royal Windsor Castle Tattoo held in the Great Park, in the shadow of Windsor Castle, and attended by the Queen and other members of the Royal Family. It was an evening event after the day's proceedings in the Royal

Windsor Horse Show. What nobody told us prior to the event was that the surface was like a ploughed field after all the horses and carriages had used it earlier in the day.

One of the largest live audiences for the Tattoo Team was the Show in the Ajax Arena in Amsterdam to celebrate the Dutch Queen Beatrix's birthday in 1998. Almost 60,000 people were entertained by Andreas Bocelli plus many other stars including Tony Hadley of Spandau Ballet. Tony was the item prior to our performance, not a bad warm-up act for us. We took fifty dancers plus three featured soloists, Gregor Bowman, Tony Cargill and Gillian Brough, with a Ceilidh Band Ensemble from the Scottish Division Lowland Military Band and Pipe Major Ian Duncan of the Vale of Atholl Pipe Band.

The Gillian Brough wing of the Ajax Stadium Display

The Duke of Edinburgh was the long-time Royal Patron of the SYHA and travelled down from Balmoral Castle to the Official Opening of the new Pitlochry Youth Hostel.

After the official unveiling of the plaque, he mixed with our Executive Members, our Senior Staff and our Guests, including many of the young people of Pitlochry who had come to see the Duke. He also had conversations with members of the SYHA Juvenile Pipe Band and complemented them on their successful competition season.

At a later date that year I was invited to take the Pipe Band and a team of dancers to a Royal Concert Celebration of Young People in the Albert Hall, London. It was a major event in the calendar with it seemed hundreds of Youth Groups performing in the show. Our section was to represent Scotland.

The SYHA Vale of Atholl Pipe Band with a Dance Team, named the Golden Eagles especially for the show, of myself plus Deryck Mitchelson, Gareth Mitchelson and Gregor Bowman (all World Champions) took to the main arena in the centre of the Albert Hall to show Scotland's traditions with a spirited Argyllshire Broadswords, complete with March On and, with formal salute to the Royal Guests, a March Off.

Dancing Through Life

In 2007 came the ultimateaccolade, I was named in the Queen's Birthday Honours List and invited to Buckingham Palace (with wife Denise plus son Kenneth and daughter Kirsty in attendance, Colin was in NZ) to be presented in the Main Ballroom to HRH Prince Charles who spoke with me for a minute or two then pinned the MBE (Member of the Order of the British Empire) on my lapel for my services to Highland Dancing around the World. Apparently, letters had been received from sponsors in different parts of the globe recommending me for an appropriate honour.

It would be remiss of me if I didn'tmention before closing this 'Royal' connections section, my Dinner with Mary, Queen of Scots, in Stirling a number of years ago.

Now he's really lost it !!!

The story is, while employed at SYHA, I had discussions about establishing a new Youth Hostel in Stirling to replace the earlier building, Argyll's Lodging, which, while a very historic building at the Top of the Town, near the Castle, was stone built, cold, a top-level historic listing and impossible to bring up to modern Youth Hostel standards.

The local Tourist Chief, James Fraser, knew this and invited me to have a meal with him to discuss the project. However, this was not just a normal meal.

At that time the Stirling Tourist Organisations had started a series of themed dinners in local historic buildings. I discovered that our discussion would take place in the ancient Guildhall, known locally as Cowane's Hospital, a property established by a Stirling Merchant, John Cowane, in 1637 as an Almshouse for elderly members of the Merchant Guildry of Stirling who had fallen on hard times. This building, which later became the Guildhall, was just metres away from Stirling Castle, where a baby Mary, Queen of Scots, at only 9 months old, was crowned in the Chapel Royal. Mary spent her early childhood in Stirling Castle and it was therefore appropriate that one of the themed dinners was billed as

'Dinner with Mary, Queen of Scots, and her Courtiers'.

It was a very successful evening of music, stories and food, eaten of course without forks, but knives were available to attack the birds and beef provided - wines were optional, and excellent. The actors and actresses playing the Queen and her Court were first class and everyone entered into the spirit of the occasion. A great night was had by all.

The result of the evening's discussions moved the new Stirling Youth Hostel project along in the right direction. James explained that the old Erskine-Marykirk church building, just down the hill, which had lain ruined for many years, could be a suitable location for SYHA and he would be happy to promote our use of it to the powers that be. The project was taken up enthusiastically by the Chairman and Executive of SYHA and a few years later a new Stirling Youth Hostel was built on that site, retaining the original church frontage which had been supported during the new build, but with a fully modern building behind it which offered magnificent views over the Back Walk at the rear, to the surrounding countryside.

My claim to fame is the new Stirling Youth Hostel came about because I had 'Dinner with Mary, Queen of Scots'. Yet another 'Royal' connection.

Through a connection in the 'My Heritage' website it seems that, some 14 generations back in my family tree, we have ancestors with direct connections to Mary, Queen of Scots. At school we all knew the song 'the Queen she had Four Marys', which includes the lines 'there was Mary Beaton and Mary Seton and Mary Carmichael and Me'.

It turns out that Mary Beaton (1543-1606) was a daughter of Robert Beaton. 4th Laird of Creich in Fife, and was one of the Four Marys who grew up with Mary Stuart and became her Ladies in Waiting. Her father, who was later to be the Master of Queen Mary's household when she returned to Scotland, travelled to France with the 5 years old Queen, her Marys and the others guarding her on her journey.

The Bethunes (or Beatons) appear in our family tree back in the 1400s and 1500s. Mary Beaton was the niece of the infamous Cardinal David Beaton, Archbishop of St Andrews, who owned Ethie Castle (near Arbroath) and was assassinated in 1546. But that is a story for another day.

After Alastair Forsyth was installed as Clan Chief in 1979 at Falkland Palace in Fife (another Forsyth connection as Stewards of the Palace) he managed to purchase Ethie Castle as his family home and we visited it on many occasions.

Spoiler: in Ethie Castle there is a stone spiral staircase from the living quarters down to Cardinal Beaton's tiny chapel.

In the dead of night, you can sometimes hear the ghost of the Cardinal (who had only one leg) bumping himself down the stair to go to pray.

My Royal Connections

31

Memories of my Young Family

Why do children have to grow up into adults? Children are impressionable, malleable, generally innocent of any malice, and accept life as it unfolds. When they 'mature' into Adults it seems they pick up so many traits that are questionable and sometimes even dangerous. They question everything and argue black is white at times. They end up with a mind of their own and, I suppose, that's a good thing.

I have many memories of activities enjoyed with my young family, pleasant, happy times where we discovered people and places and things to do where everyone could be involved and contribute.

As long as I was competing in dancing events at the Highland Games there were places to visit and journeys to make on a weekly basis during the summer. I purchased more than one old Bedford Dormobile, the converted vans which included a small stove, sink and wardrobe at the back, and seats which folded flat as benches if required, and that made it possible for us and the Neils next-door to go on adventures all over the place. Those old Dormobiles, despite visiting the local (and other) garages on a regular basis, were our lifeline to time together.

Our many trips down to the Grandparents in Nottingham were not without their problems and if it were not the Dynamo or Spark Plugs causing problems and delays it was probably the state of the Tyres. At that time our greatest asset was the AA membership which got us out of trouble on numerous occasions. Remember this was not on dual-carriageway Motorways but standard roads through towns and villages on the way. We saw the development of the A74 and M1 from regular A class roads into the Motorways of today, piece by piece, road works by roadworks.

Whether it was on our own as a family or, as happened often, joining up with our next-door neighbours for a trip away, there always seemed to be laughter and fun in the air.

The kids still talk of the journeys back from the Braemar Gatherings, down the 'Devil's Elbow' road with all its twists and turns, with the Neil brothers Angus and Jamie in the back with our three, all encouraging me to go faster over the humps on the road when the van would take off for a moment, while Anne and Margaret tried to make sandwiches and drinks in the limited space next to the cooker and sink.

It seems that generally Colin was the one to get into most trouble as he tried to do what the older boys were doing. If they were climbing trees then he would too but needed an extra push to get up into the fork of the main trunk. Only he not only got into the split in the trunk but went straight through the split and landed head-first back on the ground.

When John and Margaret, next-door, had their chimney cleaned, and had the soot in a heap on the driveway at the back door, who was it that went head first into the pile and appeared at our backdoor with only his two eyes and red hair to tell us who the apparition was?

The three of them had their own particular hobbies. With Colin it was playing football with the BB team and organising his BB drill squad that made him happy.

With Kirsty it was her involvement with the Girl Guide movement and her achievement of the premier Queens Guide Award which sailed her boat.

With Kenneth it was his love and enjoyment playing the bagpipe and travelling with his pipe band, the Vale of Atholl.

All were individual successes but they all appreciated each other's skills.

They will tell you of Easter Holidays spent at Auntie Dot's cottage. Auntie Dot was Anne's aunt, married to Grandma's brother Jack, and she had a small cottage on the cliff edge at Barmouth in Wales. As the Scottish school holidays could be before or after the Easter weekend, sometimes tourist locations were open for the season and sometimes they were not. We travelled all over that area of Wales, to Porthmadog and Portmerion, into the Snowdon National Park, on the many small-gauge railways and down the slate quarries at Blaenau Festiniog. We had long walks in the forests around Barmouth and the kids will tell you that no matter where we went, I told them there was a red telephone box just round the corner which would bring us back to the main road. There usually was a red telephone box somewhere along the walk but sometimes it didn't take us back to the main road, and we had to carry on for miles until we found it.

We took them on continental holidays with a tent on the roof rack or towing a trailer-tent behind us. I sometimes think we shouldn't have bothered as their total remembrance seems to be 'we had lunch in the Bois de Boulogne in Paris and there were chickens all over the tables at the restaurant' or 'Colin and Kirsty had sun-stroke somewhere on the beach in France, but we don't remember where'. So much for opening their eyes to the wonders of Europe. Kirsty's job on arrival in a camp site was to find the toilets, she generally needed to go anyway. Colin's was to gather information about the place and Kenneth's being the oldest was to help me set up camp.

As they grew older their friends came round to our house often, sometimes in comical circumstances. On one occasion Kenneth arrived back at the house after a night out, with Scott in tow. Scott was not too well and decided to stay the night. As usual he made for the spare bedroom and fell into bed. What he didn't know was that Auntie Pat was visiting and was already in the spare bed. Mayhem ensued as Auntie Pat screamed and thought she was being attacked and Scott, not quite with it, was not sure what was going on. A night to remember.

As late teenagers and with me still doing Cabaret evenings at Dunblane Hydro, it was a chance for them and friends to join in for a night of dancing to Jim Macleod's Band. Jim knew they would be up on the floor and helping out his visitors with some of the Scottish old-tyme dances, so everyone was a winner. Especially at Christmas and New Year when the hotel was 'resident guests only' in the ballroom, Jim would make sure that there was a table reserved for the Forsyth clan at the back of the room. While I did my stuff on the floor at 10 pm, they would encourage people during the rest of the evening to have a go at the Dashing White Sergeant, the Canadian Barn Dance and sometimes Strip the Willow.

Someone recently said to us that they go as ones, come back as twos and then in multiples, how true that is.

Memories of my Young Family

32

A Love Affair with The Cowal Highland Gathering

Cowal Highland Gathering – the venue for the Scottish and World Championships, the mecca for highland dancers from all round the world. To win one of the famous Cowal medals is always an achievement no matter what age group or which event.

The competitors come from every corner of the world to take part in the greatest test of highland dancing expertise you will ever come across. It's not just the numbers taking part which make it the highlight of the dancing year but the quality of the competition, the background and diversity of the judging panels and the concentration of dancers, teachers and adjudicators who fill the grandstands plus the volunteer stewards and scrutineers, all former dancers and teachers, who help to ensure a smooth-running and professional operation.

The Championship Trophies are a veritable history of highland dancing, with some of them first presented well over 100 years ago.

When you enter the Stadium on the first day there is a definite sense of a special occasion. The atmosphere changes, the excitement grows, the intensity of the competitors hits you, and there is a buzz which continues through the second into the third day until the World Championship Trophies are finally awarded to the jubilant successful dancers.

I first danced at Cowal as a 6 yr. old in 1947 and was awarded a 3rd place in my Sword Dance by the judge, Bobby Cuthbertson, one of highland dancing's greatest names as a dancer, teacher and judge.

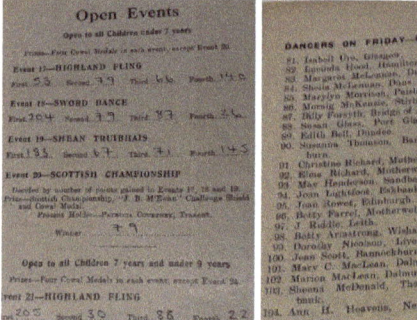 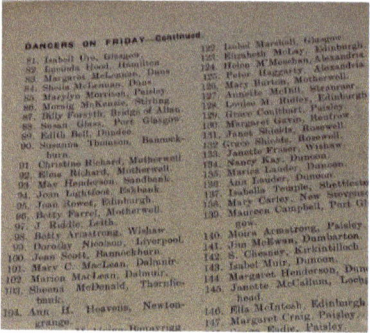

It started a love affair with Cowal which has lasted right through my dancing career.

Year after year my family made the journey to Dunoon to take part in the event, sometimes with success but many times, as a juvenile dancer, to leave empty handed. Competition was fierce and the groups could consist of up to 90 dancers so winning a medal was a real challenge. While in recent years it has been 'single age groups' in my competitive days age groups were separated by two years and the final juvenile group was under 15 years, after that you had to dance in the adult section.

In 1959 I was employed at a Chartered Accountants office in Glasgow, and I accompanied many of the senior Accountants on Company Audits. One such Audit was of Argyll County Council at their offices in Dunoon overlooking the Clyde and the old steamer pier. On a Monday morning we took the train to Gourock then the CalMac ferry over to Dunoon and walked round the bay to the Argyll C.C. Offices. There we met many of the men and women who, in addition to being local authority employees, were also involved in the running of the annual Gathering.

One of the Cowal Gathering dancing stewards at that time was Mr. Christie Park, who was one of those officers. Knowing I had been a regular at the Gathering he often talked about the organisation of the events and mentioned the mass of paperwork they required to collect, and the time taken to calculate the dancing results for all the different dances and sections, and finally list the Championship Trophy winners for the Stadium announcer to call the successful dancers to the platforms for the formal presentation of prizes and Trophies. There were, it seemed, lots of Judges listings, plus lots of transferring sheets to decide the winners of each dance, then lots of transferring sheets to bring the dance results together to decide the overall Championship winners in each age group.

I know this was long before computers became available to crunch the numbers but it was an awful lot of paper. Part of the problem was the sheer number of dancers taking part, as mentioned already, there could be up to 90 entrants for each dance and every Judge had to award a mark to each competitor.

Having considered those problems I came up with a single sheet for Judges which could take the dancers numbers, and marks awarded, for up to 90 in each individual dance. For compiling the dance results and Championship winners I combined the two elements into one sheet where each dance result was clear and the overall Championship result was produced, by simply adding together the appropriate vertical columns showing the Dance points and then the Championship points gained by each dancer who was successful in being placed by each Judge.

I passed on my suggestions to the Cowal Committee via the dancing convenor and the simpler system was implemented. While all the calculations are now carried out in a computer program which then spits out the results for the Announcer, complete with the winner's Name and home town, that basic system is the one still used at Dunoon today.

Balliemore Shield on the left, Braemar Shield, Centre & Airth Shield on Right

In the Juvenile competitions my main achievement was winning the Balliemore Shield in 1955. It was the trophy for Fourth Place in the Juvenile World Championship.

My placings in the Under 15 year's individual events had taken me through to dance in the World Finals. At that time full steps were danced in the Finals so it didn't help that I suddenly realised during the Highland Fling that I had started the last step too soon and had to repeat that last step to complete the dance. The World Championship is based on the total of placings over all the dances in the Finals so a fourth place overall was a good result given that I had shot myself in the foot in the first dance.

In 1960, 1961 and 1962 I danced in the World Championship Finals but it was 1963 before I managed to win that Title, and that day I also competed in and won the separate competition for the MacLean Trophy, the so-called Highland Dance Oscar. That was the only time it was awarded for the result of a single event, as before and since then it has always been awarded to the dancer winning most Championships over the competition year.

That World Championship win was repeated in 1964.

Sadly, the possibility of a third win in 1965 was squashed when, during my Sword Dance, when I was alone on the platform as the last competitor in the event, the heavens opened up and rain deluged the stadium.

The only people in the arena moving were myself and Pipe Major Angus Morrison, and the only other person in sight was the single Judge at our Centre Platform location trying to protect her notes from the storm. Everyone else had run for cover.

Billy & Mum with MacLean Trophy on left and World Championship Trophy

The dancing board was awash and inevitably while turning at the end of the first step, my feet skidded and down in a heap I went. No chance for a re-dance as I had chosen to start despite the looming dark clouds. So ended my quest for the hat-trick of wins.

Many years later, after I had stopped competing, I was asked if I would act as Announcer and, later still, Master of Ceremonies of the dancing events at Cowal. I have no definitive date for when I took that over as my name was not listed in the Programme for a couple of years and then was listed as one of the Dance Stewards (until 1996), however it must have been round about 1974/75 that I started calling dancers over to the platforms for their events, ensuring the programme was running smoothly and at the end of the day announcing the results. I had toured in stage shows all over Canada and the United States, performed in stage, arena and TV shows throughout the United Kingdom, competed for many years around Scotland and England, and had also judged overseas in Australia and South Africa so I was a well-known face (and voice) to most of the dancers and teachers world-wide. I had also been attending meetings of the Scottish Official Board of Highland Dancing from 1965 onwards so also had the backing and authority of the World Governing Body.

I decided in 2016 that it was time to retire from that job and allow someone new to take over. Accordingly in 2017 after 70 years of appearing on Cowal's famous platforms it was time to say goodbye. Ronnie Cairns gave me the opportunity to say a few words before the presentation of the World Championship Trophies, and typically it took me too many, rather emotional, minutes to say what Cowal, the Stadium, the Dancers, Teachers and the Cowal Committee meant to me. A video of that speech was given to me afterwards, not a pretty sight.

I was honoured with the award of an Honorary Life Patron of Cowal Gathering, which means I can return each year to witness the next stages of Cowal Gathering's journey, onwards and upwards.

33
Tracing My Family Ancestry

A number of years ago I decided that I should make an attempt at recording my family tree, basically as I knew very little about my family beyond my Grandparents in Dundonald, Fife and Bannockburn, Stirlingshire, and I thought it would be interesting for my children and their children.

I tried a few different systems and ended up subscribing to a website called MyHeritage.

With the knowledge I already had, I managed to expand the family tree a few generations and now eventually, to more than 14 generations which takes me back some 600 years to the 1400s and some really surprising connections.

On both my parent's sides of the family it appears the men have been Coal Miners, or described in some records as Coal Hewers for three generations.

I have solid information on my father's family tree going to back to John Forsyth (1822-1851) whose parents were James Forsyth and Elizabeth Clason Forsyth, but no official records yet before that.

My mother's father William Stevenson (1885-1943) may have been the illegitimate son of his mum Catherine Rew (1865-1940) as she didn't marry James Rew (1857-1915) until 1898, however on another connected family site there is the suggestion that both William and another son John Stevenson (1888- ?) were brothers of Catherine.

Beyond that I have been dependent on links from the MyHeritage website to take me back further.

When you link back to the beginning of the 1800s and earlier the family connections go far and wide.

Some of those lead to the Russell family in Clackmannan, some 9 generations back. Sir John Russell (1672-1730) of Clackmannan. Married in 1694 to Lady Janet Russell (was Colt) (1675-1718).

Even more surprising there are direct connections to the Beaton (known also as Bethune) families in Fife around the St Andrews area, including (by 15 generations) to the infamous Cardinal David Beaton who was the first Cardinal of Scotland, fought viciously against the rising tide of Presbyterianism, and was assassinated in his home, St Andrews Castle, in 1546.

This is at the time Mary, Queen of Scots, was a child and there is a further family connection to Mary Beaton (later Ogilvy) who grew up with the young Queen and became one of the Queen's Lady's in Waiting, 'the Four Mairies'. Mary's father was one of the Queen's retainers in charge of her safety on her flight to France and later Head of her Royal Household.

In those days many of the 'noble' families intermarried and one of the Beaton girls married Sir James Ogilvy, 1st Lord Ogilvy of Airlie.

I suppose it is inevitable that a Family Tree which has grown and grown for 600 years should eventually spread its branches all over Scotland and incorporate everyone from the noblest of houses to the humble Coal Hewers of this world, but doesn't it make you feel not just part of a big family but part of the history of Scotland itself.

Denise says I'm very much a 'traditionalist' and that is why I could never live permanently in another country. I would rather think of it as a privilege to be a continuation of the Scottish Cultural Stream which has given me such a varied and interesting life.

34
What advice would you give your great-grandchildren

Who am I to hand out advice, I've made as many mistakes as anyone, so here's just a few words to think about.

Take opportunities as they come

Yes, some don't work out as expected, but most do.

Never be in a position where you think 'I wish I had had a go at that'.

You never know what's possible if you don't try.

When you do try, give it everything you have, there is no point in trying if you are not going to get right into it.

It's amazing what you can do if you have belief in yourself.

I am told '97% of things you worry about never happen', so don't worry, gather all the facts and make a decision.

What advice would you give your great-grandchildren

35

On Tour with The Vale

Many, many years ago, I was asked to dance at a concert in Callander organised by one of the floor managers at STV. He advised there would be a Piper available to play for me. It turns out that the Piper was a young lad called Ian Duncan who had come along with his dad, Jock Duncan, a well-known singer of Bothy Ballads. Ian was about fourteen or fifteen years old at the time.

A few years later I was asked to dance at the series of summer Highland Nights held in the Games Park in Pitlochry as fundraisers for the local Pipe Band, the Vale of Atholl. Once again, I met Ian Duncan and his dad, plus the rest of the family. In the intervening years Ian had left school and moved on to university. The band's Pipe Major at that time was Alan Cameron, most of the band were of a similar age to Alan, it was not a competing band and played mainly for local functions and events. I was a regular competitor at Pitlochry Highland Games and kept in touch with the Vale and some of the band.

When he left University Ian was asked if he would take over as Pipe Major of the Vale from Alan Cameron, who wished to retire. Ian did so on condition that the band would start a youth policy to bring new blood into the band and would aim to enter into competitions. The competing band was mainly of fifteen- and sixteen-year-olds but in its first season did very well. In its second season, playing in Grade 4, the bottom tier of the Royal Scottish Pipe Band Association system, the Vale won all the Championship contests including the World Championship in that grade. (They were upgraded the following year to Grade 3 and Grade 2 the year after that)

Shortly afterwards Ian became a teacher of Mathematics at Crieff High School and decided to form a Juvenile section of the Band, based initially in Crieff. My son, Kenneth, had been playing pipes, taught first by Pipe Major Larry Georgeson, who had a small group of boys at Stirling Castle, then by Pipe Major Angus Macdonald (Scots Guards) whom I knew through the B.Cal Pipe Band, and eventually by top solo player Willie McCallum, who lived locally in Bridge of Allan. Kenneth was keen to join a band so we spoke to Ian and arranged to go to the Crieff practices of the new Juvenile band.

I danced at the Highland Nights for a few years and took an interest in the activities of 'The Vale'. In the year of the SYHAs 50th Anniversary the organisation sponsored the Vale Juvenile Band which played under the name 'SYHA Vale of Atholl' for a period. At one point I helped in finding a sponsor for the senior band and acted as compere for a number of the band's Concerts at home and overseas. Eventually I was called 'the band manager' only because I had assisted in those efforts.

The Vale was well known in Northern Ireland, where there is a strong history of Pipe Bands, and was asked to provide the prestigious Annual Ballymena Pipe Band Concert. With The Band as the main feature, the programme also included the Vale Small Pipes Quartet, the Vale Choir (can pipers and drummers sing?), solo spots by Gordon Duncan, a special Drum Salute from our Drum Corps, headed by Paul Turner, and a set by Ceol Beag, the folk group, headed at that time by Davy Steele, a good friend of the band. The Concert was a big success and built on the reputation of the band for innovative and modern tunes from within the tradition and from overseas as well.

As a finale 'The Vale' played a set of Gallician tunes, preceded by a solo by Gordon, on the pipes, playing the Mexican Hat Dance, and joined during the set by the Folk Group and everyone else who had been on-stage.

During the Finale the audience went wild encouraging the band to even greater efforts with the arrangements being played and the sounds being produced from the stage. It was certainly something new in the Pipe Band world. The capacity audience demanded more and to their delight 'The Vale' finished the evening with a rousing set of Reels and Jigs, once again with everyone involved, so much so that the excitement of the audience reached even the Compere (guess who that was) who joined them all on-stage, dancing along to the music, music most definitely made for dancing.

If anything, 'The Vale's' reputation was even more enhanced after that show, a resounding success all round. For the first time the Concert was recorded on Video and made available by the organisers for sale, and I understand sold out very quickly.

'The Vale' made many trips around Scotland and Overseas performing at special events and playing full concerts and joining in parades and competitions. From Tokyo and Kamagari in Japan and San Francisco in California, to Ontario, Quebec and Nova Scotia in Canada. On a separate occasion the Juvenile band, after winning the World Championship in their section, played and were featured in The Royal Nova Scotia Tattoo in Halifax and, while there, played at many venues around the province.

The story of 'The Vale's' trip to California is told elsewhere but a few words about the visits to Japan and Canada are required.

In 1989 I was asked if it was possible to bring a Pipe Band, a Scottish Dance Band and Singers and Dancers to Japan for a Festival and special week of events in Kamagari, a small Island off the south-east coast of Japan, near Hiroshima. It wasn't an easy task but eventually a group was assembled and a first-class, top-grade group it was. From Pitlochry, the Vale of Atholl Pipe Band, from Dunning, The Simon Howie Scottish Dance Band, from Perth, Gaelic singer Laura Jane Rintoul, and from the dancing world, four World Champions, Gillian Greig from Kirkcaldy, Gregor Bowman from Glasgow, Ann Milne from Owen Sound in Ontario and Jennifer Lindsay from Vancouver Island in B.C. Canada. In Japan we met up with John Freebairn, an expert on the Scottish 'Heavy' events, throwing the hammer, tossing the caber etc.

The first few days were spent in Tokyo where the band played in one of the major Shopping centres and then it was off on the 'Shinkansen', the bullet train, south to Kamagari and the Scottish Festival. The Festival covered quite an area of Kamagari with booths displaying different goods and foods from Scotland, and a stage where we could perform.

On the 'Highland Games' Day there was a wonderful display of both Japanese and Scottish culture to view.

Dancing Through Life

The Scots joined in on all the activities and even helped to carry the Shrine to a place of honour in the centre of the field, escorted of course by the Vale of Atholl Pipers playing.

In the evening a Grand Ball was held with everyone dressed up for the occasion, the girls in full-length evening dresses and the men in full dress uniform, a magnificent sight to behold.

Needless to say, after a while the jackets came off and there was a real feel of a Scottish Ceilidh. The celebrations went on well into the night and many a dram was consumed and many bottles of Saki mysteriously became empty before morning.

Talking of 'drams', the Band were invited to a meeting with the Mayor of Hiroshima and received in one of the main offices of the City and Prefecture for an 'Official Welcome'. After the Mayor spoke, I was invited to reply on behalf of the visitors, and said I was not only privileged to be there but had brought some Scottish Water as a present for the Mayor. He turned to his interpreter as if misunderstanding the words spoken, so I repeated that I had brought some Scottish Water for him, which did not make him any the wiser. His face was a big beaming smile a minute later when I presented the Scottish Water, a big bottle of a Single Malt Whisky, and he then understood what I had been talking about. He seemed very happy with his bottle of water from Scotland.

We took the opportunity, when in Hiroshima, of visiting the Peace Museum, on the site where the first Atomic Bomb was dropped in anger. I have to say that I have never before, or since, known the members of the Pipe Band to be so quiet as on that visit. It seemed that, for once, they were in awe of the significance of the site. To see first-hand the desolation caused by that bomb did strike home to everyone there. Something not to be forgotten or perhaps even forgiven.

On our return to Tokyo, via Kyoto, the ancient capital of Japan, the band played again in one of the shopping malls, but on the same day the Tokyo Highland Games were taking place so the non-playing group went along to the Games. It turned out that there was a Mini-band competition, so a few of the solo pipers came together with a couple of spare drummers and I took the Bass Drum to allow them to join the competition. At the end of the Games when the prizes were announced I was awarded the Best Bass Drum prize so I can add that to my list of achievements. Best Bass Drummer in Japan 1989.

At one point we organised a trip to the eastern Provinces of Canada and into the USA. This tour was mainly a Concert Tour arranged with different sponsors in the various locations we performed. The only competition was in Glengarry, Ontario, the site of the North American Pipe Band Championships. It was a chance for 'The Vale' to pitch against the best in North America as the band had recently been upgraded to Grade 1.

I had an interesting time trying to make sure the band were in the right place at the right time. For a while it appeared we had no Drum Corps for our Concert in Albany, New York as, despite emphasising that everyone needed a visa to enter the United States, most of the Drum Corps had not obtained one and had to be left behind in Ontario to try and get one while the rest of us went over the border to Albany. Somehow, they managed it and arrived just in time for the show.

It didn't help that the Band Secretary tried to dispose of his airline ticket after arriving in Toronto, as 'he didn't realise it had a return portion on it'. One of the Pipe Corps was quite ill in Kingston, Ontario, and had to be hospitalised there. Luckily the local Head of Surgery was a Scot and made sure he was operated on quickly (for appendicitis), or at least in time to return home with the band, albeit not as well as when he left home.

In Owen Sound a street parade had been organised and the band turned up in full No.1 dress uniform in the middle of a heatwave when all the other people in the town were in shirtsleeves order. On the beach there we had a fantastic concert with the local Highland Dancing groups joining us on stage throughout the night.

It's difficult to remember the things which went right when so much went wrong. In all of this the band went gaily on as if that was normal for them. Maybe it was!

Finally, it was during this period that 'The Vale's' recording of 'Zito the Bubbleman' went viral so, of course, that had to be celebrated with yet another Pipe Band commemorative T-shirt. My friend in The Gambia, Margaret Fell, came up with the design, and that of another T-shirt to honour 'Kenny the Sparrowman' another melody written for the Vale.

36
My proudest moment in life?

Without doubt it's a toss-up between the Winning of the World Championship for the first time in 1963 and the award of the M.B.E. (Member of the Order of the British Empire) by H.M. the Queen in 2007, in her Birthday Honours List.

I suppose, as the earlier of the two, I should choose the World Championship win but that was a one-day event, although it took a lot of hard graft prior to the day to gain the strength, flexibility and accuracy of technique the win required.

I was advised at the time that the M.B.E. was in recognition of my work for Highland Dancing Internationally and that work was done over a long number of years and in many parts of the world.

I can't split the two so they are my two Proudest Moments.

My proudest moment in life?

37
A lazy day at home?

How do I spend a lazy day at home? That's a difficult question to answer nowadays. In the past that would have been an easy one. Sleep and catch up with family and friends. When you are retired from normal employment you don't get a day off but, if like me, you have other interests then they tend to take over and you find you are involved in other activities but in a voluntary capacity.

My view however is that there is no point in stopping regular work just to spend as much time doing some other job. Retirement is there for a reason and while it may not appear like it at the time, you find that your life does slow down and your reactions in thought and in action do tend to be slower as well. It is also true that taking a little extra time to make decisions is not a bad idea.

I was told many years ago that in the Banking business, the Bank Managers who take up the option to retire at age 60 live to a ripe old age, but the Managers who carry on until mandatory retirement at age 65 tend not to live beyond age 70. Whether because of the stress of such responsibility or other reasons, why take the chance.

I retired from my CEO position a few years early because I had been financially careful in my earlier years, and I had other interests which would keep me occupied, but on a part-time basis.

My involvement with the Royal Edinburgh Military Tattoo, the Royal Scottish Official Board of Highland Dancing, some Championship and Competition Judging jobs at home and

A lazy day at home?

overseas, plus occasionally Consulting, Hosting and Compering dancing events kept me in touch without becoming too tiring.

So now its feet up, TV on, mainly Sports events, particularly Olympic or other major Athletics Championships, or in football Scottish, European and World Cups or, failing all else, Track and Road Cycling, but not under any circumstances Cricket. There's a theme there – competition and constant activity.

I still enjoy reading and a few years ago transferred from hard and soft backed books to reading on my Kindle, which was a much-appreciated present from the girls after my last night at the Royal Edinburgh Military Tattoo. From psychological thrillers to crime stories of all kinds, procedural, courtroom drama and mysterious circumstances. Can I work out 'who dunnit' before the end. Rarely.

I do have a rule, however about activities, 'Try to avoid any activity on a Monday.'

If I can't have a day off at least I can keep Monday as a quiet day.

38

The country has changed during my lifetime

In the computer semi-conductor industry, it is said that the power of those processors has doubled every two years, and at a much lower production cost (Moore's Law). It seems to me that the changes in how we live are accelerating, maybe not to that level, but faster and faster as time goes on.

As a child of the 1940s, our living standards then were basic, but in most cases, sufficient for our needs at the time. Or at least we thought so then. We didn't realise that there were all those material things which we needed and which we needed immediately. Bigger homes, newer furnishings, a wider variety of clothes and of foodstuffs, and more entertainment systems for the house.

When football matches first were broadcast on TV, I remember asking Mr. Scott, across the road, if I could visit him and watch the game on his new 14-inch screen sitting in its big wood-finished cabinet in the corner of his sitting room.

Now it seems people have 'Cinema' rooms, specially laid out to watch TV programmes and Movies on 60', 70' and 80' screens, broadcast on the internet by hundreds and hundreds of online channels.

The country has changed during my lifetime

As an Adult I dutifully travelled for years through to Edinburgh every two months or so to the regular meetings of the RSOBHD. Since the major upgrades in communications after the Covid 19 pandemic, we can now hold meetings incorporating all our affiliated member bodies around the world from the comfort of our own home through the wonder of Skype or Zoom programmes.

The first time I travelled to London was in 1951, on a supporters bus organised by Stirling Albion fans, for the Scotland versus England football match at the old Wembley Stadium. We left Stirling at 5.45 pm on Friday afternoon, stopped in Penrith for Supper at the Queens Head Hotel, and arrived at the Victoria Coach Station in London on the Saturday morning at 8 am.

The modern roads network means you can travel all the way from the Dunblane roundabout to London on dual carriageways or Motorways, and be there in about 7 hours and that is allowing for a meal stop halfway.

My first trip in an aeroplane was a big adventure to Douglas on the Isle of Man and we travelled in a big box like aircraft from the old Renfrew Airport. Now Central Scotland has three major International Airports with regular direct flights to Scandinavia, Europe, the Middle East, Canada and the United States. There are also hundreds of Holiday Flights to the Mediterranean countries taking off, it appears, every day for families to enjoy the sun. A few years ago, one of my friend's daughters, she was about 7 yrs. old, was complaining that she had never flown to Spain on holiday and all her classmates had been there. Such is the modern child.

Whereas in our early car travelling days there was little traffic on the roads (and we could run our carts down the pavement of the Station Brae) today there are regular tailbacks from the Dunblane roundabout down almost into Bridge of Allan, waiting to join the motorway system.

Although it definitely has its benefits in keeping friends, and particularly families, in touch with each other, the rubbish posted by self-appointed experts on systems like Facebook, Instagram etc. could cause riots in an empty room. Every opinionated individual with a view can broadcast their conspiracy theories, and the problem is that there are many thousands out there who will believe them.

I would love to say that my younger days were spent in blissful cold, snow-bound winters and bright sunny summers, but has the weather actually changed over the last fifty years or so? I don't know and I'll leave those sorts of statements to others more qualified than me.

For my money the major changes in Scotland over my lifetime, and all for the better, are the ones which have improved the health of my countrymen and women. New medical devices and equipment, innovations in treatment linked to modern drug discoveries are changing completely the health of Scots. Slowly but surely, we are being persuaded to live healthier lives, and boy is it needed.

For myself, I would not still be here without the fantastic services provided by our Scottish National Health Service, and that is true of my family as well. Whether for routine ops like tonsils or more complicated ones like drug eluting stents, or the benefits of baby incubators and ventilators and breathing machines, our Scottish National Health Service is one of the greatest successes of our time and should be resourced and funded to a level commensurate with its benefits to the Nation.

We have come from the early days of land and air travel to the exploration of space and the stars in a very short period, now our latest generation 'will boldly go where no man has gone before' to quote Captain James T. Kirk.

Now we need to have the confidence to take over the organisation and operation of our country ourselves, where the successes are because of our endeavours and any problems that arise are accepted, addressed and funded by us.

I'm definitely my Mother's son and vote accordingly.

39

Memorable Favourite Trips

If I ignore the USA/Canada coast to coast tours which started me off on overseas trips then there are four others which stand out. Only one was a single visit, the others being a series of visits over a period of years, but all came about indirectly as a result of my involvement with the Royal Edinburgh Military Tattoo and the Royal Scottish Official Board of Highland Dancing.

In 2012 I was invited to take my Highland Ceilidh Dancers team to perform at the Royal Oman Military Music Festival, on this occasion celebrating the 50th year of the Sultan's reign. The invitation requested a team of 50 dancers to perform a twelve-minute spot in the programme with the proviso also that the music would be played by the Royal Omani Forces, incorporating both Pipe Bands and Military Bands.

In the Royal Edinburgh Military Tattoo we were generally limited to a performance of around five minutes so a new enhanced routine was developed for the show. For our accompaniment my Piper son Kenneth set up the music score and liaised with the Musical Director of the Oman show (a former member of the Scots Military Ceilidh Band), who wrote the arrangement for his Omani Military musicians, including Pipers. Those Pipers, incidentally, were members of the only Mounted Pipe Band in the World, not on horseback, but on specially bred and trained Camels. On this occasion, of course, they were not mounted but playing alongside the other musicians in the pit orchestra for the show.

The trip was spectacular in many ways. It was a city which none of us would ever visit under normal circumstances. The venue for the Music Festival was a specially built arena formed in the courtyard and outdoor square precinct of the Royal Opera House in Muscat, the capital of Oman.

While there the girls expressed a wish to see Camels and to everyone's delight, we were invited by the Brigadier in charge of our trip, to visit the Sultan's camel ranch where they bred and trained them. We were met there on arrival by some of the Mounted Pipe Band who played for us as we dismounted from the coach. Lots of photographs were taken and the team were given a chance to ride on camels brought out of the stables for the visit.

After a tour of the complex, as a bonus we were then taken to the Sultan's racecourse and stables where his thoroughbreds were trained for the major horse races around the world, and his collection of carriages were housed. A chance mention of 'the pink stallion' led to the news that it had just returned from Europe where it was stabled over the summer to avoid the Omani heat. The Sultan's trainer sent one of his staff to bring it forward and a few of us were able to see this magnificent stallion whose coat was a unique sort of rose gold colour.

If the members of that team remembered the visit to Muscat, I'm sure that the traders in the local Muscat 'souks' remembered them as well. It looked as if the girls had cleared their stocks of Harem Pants (nicknamed Camel pants) with the quantity they brought back to Scotland. They had combed the hundreds of narrow alleyways and passages of the souks, buying up all sorts of souvenirs to take home with them. All the local traders were familiar with the Scottish Girls who kept buying up their stocks.

Our series of visits to Japan was to take part in a Scottish Festival at a fantastic Swiss mountain style hotel in the heart of the Japanese Alps to the west of the country near Nanaimo, which was the main location for the Winter Olympics when they were held in Japan.

Those visits were organised through the auspices of my good friend, Masako Okada Naitoh (Marchand) whom I had first met on a British Week Export Mission to Tokyo away back in 1969. I had visited Japan a number of times, judging the highland dancing competitions at the Tokyo Highland Games and in 1989 had led a very large group to a Scottish Festival in Kamagari (an island near Hiroshima). I had also visited with the Atholl Highlanders in 1987 and brought a team of Japanese Highland Dancers to the Glasgow Garden Festival in 1988.

I had many friends and contacts in Japan through the Scottish Dance community and through organisations such as the Japan Scotland Society and the St Andrews Society. I was therefore well known amongst the Scottish dancing community in Japan, so when in 2009 I was asked if I would bring to a Festival in Hakuba some of the younger members of the Highland Ceilidh Dancers team I was delighted to agree.

After many years of travelling all over Europe and even to Canada and Australia, many of the older girls had performed overseas, particularly in Germany, the Netherlands, and Switzerland so this trip gave the newer, younger dancers a chance to travel to a new country.

For six years in succession Denise and I took four of the younger dancers to visit the 'Land of the Rising Sun'. It was a completely new experience for them and a complete contrast to life in Scotland, but they took it in their stride. On the first trip one of the girls had just been awarded Black Belt level in Judo back home in Kirkcaldy, so we arranged for her to visit a store in Tokyo where she could purchase her actual Black Belt in the home of Judo.

It was a great experience for the young dancers whose performances were so appreciated by the Japanese dancers and the expatriate Scots who came to the event. Even the six-hour car journey from Tokyo added interest through the varied countryside and different small regional towns we passed. In Hakuba the girls danced solo and joined with some Japanese Highland dancers in performing Strathspeys and Reels.

The hotel served meals in a mixture of Far East, Western and European style, but it was mandatory (by me) that the girls tried eating with chopsticks and some typical Japanese foods. The hotel had the most wonderful staircases, reminiscent of the Harry Potter staircases at Hogwarts, his school. If they had started moving back and forward on their own, I don't think we would have been surprised.

We had a full day in Tokyo before returning home so apart from a visit to the 'shopping street', hundreds of small stalls full of souvenirs, where did the girls want to go? No contest, they had noticed a sign for Tokyo Disneyland on the drive in from the airport so that was the destination.

When the first group returned to Scotland and told the others, the groups for the five following years of course demanded the same last day visit. Although every sign was in Japanese that didn't stop them all having the time of their lives on all the rides.

A bit closer to home, in 2008 I was asked if a tour operator, who specialised in group trips to Disneyland Paris, could visit and talk to me about a project he was considering. As a result a few of us sat round the giant table in the old farmhouse kitchen at Easter Greenyards in Dunblane, discussing whether it would be a good idea to operate a long weekend for Highland Dance Schools in Disneyland Paris. It would include, obviously, access tickets to the Disney Parks plus a Showcase opportunity for each school to perform a 10-minute programme of their own choice, visits to the event venue from Disney Characters and a Scottish Ceilidh on the Saturday night. The big attraction however would be a chance to take part in a specially choreographed 'Pre-Parade' along the famous Disney Parade Route through the park, moving off about 45 minutes before the main Disney Parade – hence the 'Pre-Parade' designation. Can you imagine the opportunity to savour the excitement and boisterous applause of the amazing crowds lined up on each side of the route as they were awaiting the main parade.

My role was to advise on the programme for the weekend, host the Showcase and generally comment on the suggestions from the others involved. Originally it was agreed to pull in another Dance Teacher to choreograph the Official Opening of the weekend and the Pre-Parade 'dance', a simple, moving forward script, which all the dancers (ages from 7 upwards) could manage to perform. As things turned out, circumstances meant I had to do both myself, which caused some late nights and lots of instructions being written out and distributed to the dance teachers.

A total of almost thirty Highland Dance Schools signed up to the weekend with over three hundred dancers plus Mums, Dads, Grannies and Friends joining in the festivities, well over 500 people in total attending. For the Showcase and the Ceilidh we were allocated a large tented arena behind the Star Tours attraction in the Discoveryland sector of the Park.

For the Official Opening we had organised a visit from Mickey and Minnie but the dancers were not aware of that. Two dancers from each school were invited to be part of the choreographed Opening and, when all the schools had been introduced, they stayed on stage as our Guests of Honour were invited into the tent and through the teams of dancers up to the front. To see the faces of the younger dancers was an absolute delight as Mickey and Minnie made their way to the stage.

At that point we had the selected dancers form a circle and dance a Barn Dance. Surprise, surprise, Mickey and Minnie were not content with just watching and insisted on joining in with the Barn Dance.

As we had arranged that it be Progressive, all the dancers onstage had the opportunity to partner either Mickey or Minnie as they went round. It was a great success and a great start to the weekend.

In later years a Highland Competition was added to the programme and a ChoreoMagic Competition, a freestyle event using Disney Music, where the dancers could use their skills in Highland to feature a new routine using their favourite tunes and songs from the Disney catalogue. The ChoreoMagic section was judged by Disney personnel and the prizes awarded symbolised the Disney theme of the weekend.

Unfortunately, as with many other events, everything ground to a halt because of the Covid Pandemic and it has been difficult to get everything up and running again. I'm sure, however, that the wonderfully named 'Take Us 2 the Magic' company will be aiming to resurrect the weekends which so many Dancers, Parents and Friends have enjoyed for the last ten years.

There is one more location which I should mention in this section which is not a one-off trip but a continuing series of trips which has been one of the constants in my life for many years. The town of Oban, on Scotland's west coast, has hosted an annual cultural festival for forty years under the name The Highlands and Islands Music and Dance Festival (HIMDF) covering competitions in Highland Dance, Piping, Fiddle, Woodwind and Brass, Piano, Clarsach, Accordion and Singing.

Although Oban has a population of only around 8,000, during the summer months there can be about 24,000 visitors passing through the town as it is known as 'The Gateway to the Isles'. It is an important ferry point for islands of the Inner and Outer Hebrides and the hub for the many Caledonian McBrayne services to the islands.

In 1992 I was approached by James McCorkindale, the dance teacher in Campbeltown, about an idea he had concerning the Festival. The organising committee had asked for some ideas on how to differentiate the Festival from all the others around Scotland and James had suggested two possibilities, which the committee had accepted provided that James was one of the organisers of them. Highland Dancing is very much a solo activity and James wanted to hold an event which brought dancers together in competition. He wanted to run a competition which included dancers from various parts of Scotland representing their home area, and suggested that some of the current area confined events winners be invited to Oban as a team to compete against other area teams to see which area was the Top Highland Dancing Area of Scotland.

Thus was born the Scottish Area Finals with teams from 32 different areas around the country competing against one another for the Title. Although the dancers were competing as individuals, the points won by each dancer (using the Championships points system) were added together into a total for their team to provide the overall result.

The Scottish Area Finals is still the only Highland Dance Team Competition in the world.

At the same time, as an alternative to the standard Highland competitions, James had put forward a suggestion that the Festival organise a 'Choreography Challenge' where dance teachers could enter a team of their students in a freestyle event where the dancers could use their skills in Highland to feature a new routine on a theme set by the Festival. This too had been accepted and it became the biggest Highland Choreography competition in the world.

Their many themes over the years have included, An Event in Scottish History, A Place in Scotland, A Day at the Games, Sport in Scotland, Tourism in Scotland, Robert Burns, Promote Something Scottish, New York Tartan Day, The Scottish Parliament and a Scottish Theme to a piece of music set by the Festival.

Where do I fit into this picture? Well, I had acted as Host and Compere at various events at home and overseas so James asked if I would also act as the Announcer and Host at the Area Finals and Choreography events in Oban.

Thirty years later I am still acting as the Announcer and Host of those events and delighted to do so.

On the May Bank Holiday weekend, we set off on our journey to Oban and, as there is really only one main road from central Scotland into Oban. we are part of a cavalcade of cars full of dancers and friends making their way from north, south, east and west for our annual weekend in the Highland town. For a few days Oban is taken over by Dancers and Pipers and many other musicians and while the younger ones are put to bed at a 'reasonable' hour the adults can enjoy the restaurants, bars and ceilidhs that Oban has to offer.

Part of the idea behind the Festival was to encourage people on the islands to be a part of the event and many deals have been done with local businesses and the transportation companies (mainly Calmac and West Coast Motors) to make sure that they are able to take part. It is not easy for islanders to attend competitions around Scotland and HIMDF makes sure that they can get to the Oban events and consider the timetables when setting up times for competitions.

Once again Covid 19 caused the Festival to cancel the 2020 and 2021 events but I'm pleased to say that the dancing and piping events are back up and running again and plans are in place to add the others sections when finance allows.

Life would not be the same without the annual trip to Oban and thanks are due to James, Kelly Grassick, Margaret Farmer (Treasurer) and the Sinclair family for all the work they do to ensure everyone has a great time. It is probably not generally known that Neil Sinclair and his wife Sheila were involved at the very beginning of the Festival along with the Festival Patron, Mrs. Frances Shand Kidd (Princess Diana's mother) who was a local resident. Neil and Sheila passed on their duties to other members of the family and their daughter, Isla Munro, with the help of her family, is keeping the tradition going, as she has now been Convenor and Organiser of the Dancing events for many years.

Here's hoping there are many HIMDFs still to enjoy.

40
How should I be Remembered?

It's not up to me to say how I will be remembered, there are enough people out there who have known me for a very long time and can comment on what I've done, or not done, over the years, particularly in the Highland Dance world.

How I would want to be remembered is slightly different and everyone likes to think they have made some small difference in this world.

In my case I have been involved in Highland Dancing all my life and would like to think that during that time I have learned that, in the words of the old saying 'you can't please all of the people all of the time'. I chaired the RSOBHD meetings for many years and believe that I had to be a hands-off Chairman, listening to all opinions, looking for compromise on all sides, and trying to guide the Board to a conclusion that everyone could accept.

One of the reasons I was asked to be Chairman (and later President) was, at that time, I was not a paid-up member of any of the Examining Bodies (I had been a member of the HDSA, long defunct) and was considered to be 'Independent' and without bias on behalf of any of them. As an individual I probably made no difference as such, but guided the RSOBHD to conclusions which definitely did make a difference to the Highland Dance Community and definitely to the organisations involved in it world-wide.

As a Libran (born 5 October) I have always looked at both sides of any question so that I could see where the benefits and problems might be. I have taken that approach into my business career and

How should I be Remembered?

it has served me well there. At times I have had to make serious decisions affecting many people, their lives and families and I hope I have been fair and transparent when doing so.

In my private life things have not always gone well but I have a family of 16 grandchildren plus numerous nephews and nieces (blood relatives and others) most of whom come to see me occasionally, plus of course, their parents, who seem to tolerate my idiosyncrasies.

A long time ago I came across the Latin expression 'Facta non Verba' or in English 'Deeds not Words'. It seems to me if more people got on with the job instead of spending hours talking about it, we would all be better off.

So I hope that it will be said he was fair but honest in his life and tried to do his best for as many as he could.

41
A Timeline

1940 William Blair Stevenson Forsyth, date of birth 05 October (William Blair after my grandfather plus Stevenson, my mother's maiden name)

1944 Started dance classes with Margaret Mason in Keirfield Cottages, Bridge of Allan.

1947 Moved to a new house at 20 Cawder Gardens, Bridge of Allan.

Cowal Highland Gathering, 3rd place medal in Sword Dance

1950 Airth Highland Games - Cuthbertson Shield for Boys (also 1952 to 1956)

1951 Started Highland lessons with Willie Cuthbertson 27th June

1953 Winner Scottish Boys Championship (also in 1954 & 1956)

1954 St Andrews Hall, Glasgow Concert with Robert Wilson/Will Starr/Sydney Devine

1955 Cowal Gathering – 4th in Juvenile World Championship, Balliemore Shield.

Braemar Gathering – Boys Championship Cup –

invited to dance Solo for H.M. Queen

1956 Dunblane Highland Society Concert with Kenneth McKellar

A Timeline

1958 SOBHD Team representing Scotland at the International Military Tattoo in Dublin.

Holyrood Palace Royal Visit

1958 Scottish International Highland team

1959 Carroll Levis Show, Empire Theatre, Glasgow

1960 'Caledonia' first transcontinental tour of USA and Canada

1961 STV Jigtime series Theatre Royal, Glasgow, Dance Director Bruce McClure.

Holyrood Palace Royal Visit

1961 Scottish International Highland team.

STV Hogmanay Programme

1962 'Caledonia' 2nd transcontinental tour of USA and Canada.

Summer Season at the Cragburn Pavilion, Gourock with Margaret Gordon.

'Hail Caledonia' Indoor Highland Games, Kelvin Hall

1963 Winner of the Adult World Highland Dance Championship.

Winner of the MacLean Trophy for best Adult Dancer of the year.

Dance Director STV Hogmanay Party from Theatre Royal, Glasgow

1964 Dance Director new TV series The Jimmy Blair Band Show.

Winner Adult World Highland Dance Championship for second time.

Perth Theatre, 'Highland Fling' Guest Spot, with Aly Wilson, Alexander Brothers

1965 Southern California Highland Dancing Association representative at the RSOBHD Meetings.

Various Venues throughout Scotland with Allan Water Dancers.

Dance Director STV Hogmanay Party from Theatre Royal, Glasgow

1966 Married to Anne Metheringham (16/10/1944 – 12/04/2016) Beeston, Nottingham

1967 Moved to Donbros Knitwear at Lornshill, Alloa.

Kenneth Iain Forsyth born 12th March

1968 Kirsty Anne Forsyth born 10th September,

Colin Andrew Forsyth born 11th September

Twins born on different days 11.30 pm and 00.05 am

1969 McVities Highland Games, Tokyo Japan, part of British Week

1971 McVities Highland Games, San Francisco USA, part of British Week

1973 UNICEF Concert, City Halls, Glasgow, with Peter Morrison/ Alasdair Macdonald etc.

Jamie's Cabaret, King James Hotel, Edinburgh, with Larry Marshall & Kay Rose.

Elected Chairman SOBHD

1974 Jamie's Cabaret, King James Hotel, Edinburgh, with Larry Marshall & Kay Rose

1975 Moved, as Accountant, to Scottish Youth Hostels Association HQ in Stirling

1977 Central Region Exchange Visit to Odenwald, Germany, with James Anderson, Council Convenor

1978 Scotland at the London Boat Show in January

1981 British Caledonian Airways – Inaugural Flights to Puerto Rico and Ecuador, plus The Gambia, Sierra Leone, Senegal, Mexico and Houston / Atlanta / Dallas / Fort Worth / Los Angeles in USA

1986 P&O Cruises, CANBERRA with Jim MacLeod and his Band. Judge at Tokyo Highland Games

1987 Scottish Tourism Promotion to Japan with Atholl Highlanders.

Judge at Tokyo Highland Games

A Timeline

1989 Tokyo/Kamagari Highland Gatherings, Japan
1992 Royal Edinburgh Military Tattoo, with Scottish Country Dancers
1993 Royal Edinburgh Military Tattoo, with Scottish Country Dancers
1994 Royal Edinburgh Military Tattoo, with Scottish Country Dancers
1995 Royal Edinburgh Military Tattoo, with Scottish Country Dancers
1996 Royal Edinburgh Military Tattoo, with Scottish Country Dancers
1997 Royal Edinburgh Military Tattoo, The Highland Ceilidh Dance
1998 Royal Edinburgh Military Tattoo, The Scots/Irish year
1999 Royal Edinburgh Military Tattoo, The Solo Drummer & Dancer.

The Berwick Tattoo, REMT Dancers and the Scottish Division Lowland Military Band,

Ajax Arena, Amsterdam, Queen Beatrix's Birthday Concert, REMT Group with Ceilidh Band

2000 Royal Edinburgh Military Tattoo, the Dougie Maclean 'Perthshire Amber' Dance.

Royal Edinburgh Military Tattoo in Wellington,

New Zealand

2001 Royal Nova Scotia Tattoo, Halifax Canada.

The Berwick Tattoo, REMT Dancers and the Scottish Division Lowland Military Band.

Scottish Youth Hostels Association – Retired as Chief Executive after 26 years with SYHA

2002 Queen's Golden Jubilee Royal Edinburgh Military Tattoo, Commonwealth Team.

Glasgow Scottish Tattoo in the Glasgow Royal Concert Hall.

United Kingdom Alliance Centenary Ball, Blackpool.

Duke of Edinburgh Reception at Edinburgh Castle with Pipes and Drums of The Highlanders

2003 Royal Edinburgh Military Tattoo, 'The Sword Dance of the Great Wheels'.

Northern Ireland RSPBA Championships, Banbridge.

St Andrews Night Concert, Belfast.

2004 Royal Edinburgh Military Tattoo, the 'Wings' Dance year.

New Scottish Parliament Building the Official Opening

2005 Royal Edinburgh Military Tattoo, the 'Sailing' Dance year.

Married Ann Denise Lindsay in Queen Margaret Chapel, Edinburgh Castle.

HRH Princes Royal with the Tattoo Production team.

Royal Edinburgh Military Tattoo 'A Salute to Australia' in Sydney, NSW.

The 'Netherlands National Taptoe', 's-Hertogenbosch.

RSPBA County Down Championships, Castle Ward N.I.

'Highland Spring' Reception & Dinner (London) for retired Scottish Rugby legend Kenny Logan

2006 Royal Edinburgh Military Tattoo, the 'Battle' Dance.

The Basel Tattoo, Switzerland,

2007 Royal Edinburgh Military Tattoo, the Queen's Diamond Jubilee Dance year.

60th Anniversary India's Independence Function in Glasgow.

The 'Netherlands National Taptoe', Rotterdam.

Fulda (Germany) International Tattoo.

Fort George (Inverness) Military Tatto

2008 Royal Edinburgh Military Tattoo, the Canadian Emigrants Dance.

A Timeline

Stirling Military Show, Armed Forces Day.

52 Brigade Reception, Edinburgh Castle.

United Kingdom Alliance – Annual Conference (Blackpool).

World Cross-Country Championships (Edinburgh).

Olympia (London) Military Display

2009 Royal Edinburgh Military Tattoo, the Tam o' Shanter Dance.

Royal Windsor Horse Show and Tattoo (Windsor Castle).

Fulda (Germany) International Tattoo. Japan/Scotland Festival, Hakuba, Japan.

2010 Royal Edinburgh Military Tattoo, Celebrating the Tattoo's 60 Years.

Voorthuizen (Netherlands) Military Tattoo.

Japan/Scotland Festival, Hakuba, Japan.

International Rugby (Murrayfield) Over 100 Highland Dancers.

Assemble and Leap Celebration of 60 years of RSOBHD

2011 Royal Edinburgh Military Tattoo, the Fishy Dance.

Japan/Scotland Festival, Hakuba, Japan.

International Gathering of Scottish Highland Dance, Disneyland Paris.

Usher Hall, Edinburgh Remembrance Concert

2012 Royal Edinburgh Military Tattoo, the Whisky Dance.

Japan/Scotland Festival, Hakuba, Japan.

Garmisch Partenkirchen Tattoo, Germany.

International Gathering of Scottish Highland Dance, Disneyland Paris

2013 Royal Edinburgh Military Tattoo, the 'Final Salute'.

Japan/Scotland Festival, Hakuba, Japan.

International Gathering of Scottish Highland Dance, Disneyland Paris.

2014 Across the Board with Highland Dancing, Paisley Town Hall.

Japan/Scotland Festival, Hakuba, Japan.

International Gathering of Scottish Highland Dance, Disneyland Paris.

Oman Military Music Festival, Opera House Square, Muscat, Sultanate of Oman

2015 International Gathering of Scottish Highland Dance, Disneyland Paris

2016 International Gathering of Scottish Highland Dance, Disneyland Paris.

Elected Hon. President RSOBHD again

2017 International Gathering of Scottish Highland Dance, Walt Disney World Florida USA.

Re-elected Hon. President, RSOBHD.

International Gathering of Scottish Highland Dance, Disneyland Paris.

Across the Board with Highland Dancing, Greenock Arts Theatre.

International Gathering of Scottish Highland Dance, Walt Disney World Florida USA .

2018 Re-elected Hon. President, RSOBHD

International Gathering of Scottish Highland Dance, Disneyland Paris

2019 Re-elected Hon. President, RSOBHD

International Gathering of Scottish Highland Dance, Disneyland Paris

2020 Covid 19 Pandemic closed everything down for a while. Re-elected Hon. President, RSOBHD

2021 Re-elected Hon. President, RSOBHD

2022 Re-elected Hon. President, RSOBHD

A Timeline

42

The Author

Billy Forsyth M.B.E. is a well-recognised name, face and voice throughout the Scottish Highland Dance world due to his involvement for over 70 years in competitions, adjudication, administration and promotion of Highland Dancing.

Billy was the annually elected RSOBIID Chairman from 1973 until 1996, served as President from 1997 until 2006 and was in 2008 appointed an Honorary Member of SOBHD.

He has been listed on the RSOBHD Judges Panel for more than fifty years.

He was awarded an MBE (Member of the Order of the British Empire) in the 2007 Queen's Birthday Honours List for services to Highland Dancing Internationally.

In 2016 he was asked by the three UK Examining Bodies to stand again for the position of RSOBHD President and was duly elected

The Author

at the 2016 SOBHD AGM and at the subsequent Annual General Meetings to date.

Twice winner of the World Highland Dancing Championship, Billy has extensive experience as Performer, Manager and Director of Stage, Arena, Cabaret and Network Television shows in Scotland and around the world. He has adjudicated at dance Championships on every continent, toured and performed across Canada and the United States, and demonstrated and lectured in such diverse locations as Tokyo, Japan, Quito in Ecuador and Karachi, Pakistan.

For 22 years until 2013 he was Highland Dance Director for the world-famous Royal Edinburgh Military Tattoo and through it provided opportunities for many home and overseas dancers to take part in the show. In addition to the 'Highland Ceilidh Dancers' team in Scotland he arranged for invitations from the Tattoo Producers to guest teams organised by dance teachers from Australia, Canada, New Zealand and South Africa.

Billy is recognised as the International Voice of Highland Dancing, Hosting and acting as Master of Ceremonies at many Championships (including the World Championships) and Stage Shows and has also provided dancers and dance teams for many events in Scotland and Overseas, in particular throughout Europe and in Canada, Australia and New Zealand.

Prior to retirement Billy was Chief Executive of Scottish Youth Hostels (Hosteling International Scotland) which at the time registered over 600,000 overnight visits per year and was the largest network of holiday accommodation in Scotland specially provided for young people and outdoor enthusiasts.

www.ingramcontent.com/pod-product-compliance
Lightning Source LLC
Chambersburg PA
CBHW041137110526
44590CB00027B/4048